PUBLICATION OF THE AMERICAN DIALECT SOCIETY

Number 5

A GLOSSARY
OF VIRGINIA WORDS

By

PHYLLIS J. NIXON

WITH A PREFACE BY
HANS KURATH

THE SECRETARY'S REPORT

Published by the
AMERICAN DIALECT SOCIETY
May, 1946

Obtainable from the Secretary of the Society
Woman's College of the
University of North Carolina
Greensboro, North Carolina

OFFICERS

OF

THE AMERICAN DIALECT SOCIETY

Continued on Cover 3

PUBLICATION OF THE AMERICAN DIALECT SOCIETY

Number 5

A GLOSSARY
OF VIRGINIA WORDS

By
PHYLLIS J. NIXON

WITH A PREFACE BY
HANS KURATH

THE SECRETARY'S REPORT

Published by the
AMERICAN DIALECT SOCIETY
May, 1946

Obtainable from the Secretary of the Society
Woman's College of the
University of North Carolina
Greensboro, North Carolina

PREFACE

This glossary of Virginia words, by Phyllis Jones Nixon, though modest in scope, is a contribution to our knowledge of the Virginia vocabulary in more than one way.

First of all, 39 words that have not previously been booked for Virginia make their appearance:

coal scuttle	lay (of wind)
corn stack, "crib"	milk gap
doney	old-fields colt
dry-land frog, "toad"	paling fence
egg bread	pert
fishing worm	piece, piece meal
flannel cake	poke
foreigner	proud, "pleased"
freshen	pull flowers
gentleman cow	red-worm
ground worm	rock fence
guano sack	saw buck
hand irons	(sea) grass sack
hay cock	side meat
hay doodle	smear case
hommy	somerset
hunkers	stairsteps
jam across	trumpery
johnny house	woods colt
lamp oil	

Six of these, *corn stack*, *dry-land frog*, *grass sack*, *johnny house*, *milk gap*, and *old-fields colt*, have never been recorded in any dictionary or word list, either American or British, *lamp oil* only in the NED.

These numbers are not impressive in themselves. However, when we take into account the fact that Green's *Virginia Word Book* is the best regional glossary we possess in the field of American English, and that the *Linguistic Atlas*, from which these words were culled, merely samples the vocabulary to determine types of regional distribution, we are forcefully made aware of the wealth of regional and local vocabulary that awaits the hand of the lexicographer.

3

Mrs. Nixon's second contribution is in the nature of an innovation in American lexicography. She tells us briefly whether a word is current in all of Virginia or only in a part of it; whether it is used on all social levels, or restricted to the cultured or the simple folk; whether it is in common use or rare. Such statements can be made only when a systematic survey of an area has been carried out. But this type of information is of the greatest importance. Speech areas can be delimited in no other way, and the history of individual expressions in North America can be traced only in relation to settlement history, the growth of centers of trade and culture, the development of transportation facilities, etc. It is obviously essential to know whether a Virginia word is found only in the Tidewater area, or the Valley, or the Piedmont, or in any combination of such subareas, before one can undertake to relate its history to the history of the population. A good dictionary of American English should, therefore, provide this type of information. Such broad labels as "Southern" and "Western" have little significance.

About 40 per cent of the words in this glossary are not to be found in the recently completed *Dictionary of American English*. Many of these words are current not only in Virginia but in large parts of the South and the South Midland, some of them also in the North Midland and the North, e.g. the food terms *clabber cheese, green-beans, hasslet, pully-bone, snack;* the farm words *change, cut, boar hog, freshen, nicker, whinny, stud horse, rick,* and *bundle* ("sheaf"); names for things around the house such as *burlap sack, lamp oil, poke, spicket, whet-rock;* the weather terms *abate, bluster up, calm down, moderate, rise, squall;* and such expressions as *favor* ("resemble"), *kin folks, kin to, song ballad, woods colt.* Other items omitted from the DAE are more local in character or humble folk words, e.g. *base-born, buss, doney, doodle* ("hay cock").

All words in this glossary that have not found a place in the *Dictionary of American English* are labeled with an asterisk to emphasize the need of a *Dictionary of Spoken American English* to supplement the DAE, which is based almost entirely on printed sources. What we need is not a Dialect Dictionary in the narrow sense of the word but a full record of the vocabulary of spoken English in its regional and local manifestations and its social variations in which not only the meanings but also the geographic and social spread of each word are defined. The intimate tie-up between regional and local vocabulary and features of regional and local culture cannot be visualized in any other way; and, in turn, a history of the American vocabulary cannot be written until we shall know both the words and the things they denote.

The procedure that should be followed in the preparation of a *Dictionary of Spoken American English* would seem to be quite obvious.

We must have, first of all, comprehensive glossaries of the everyday vocabulary of carefully chosen active focal areas such as Eastern Massachusetts, the lower Connecticut Valley, the Hudson Valley, Delaware Bay, the Pittsburgh area, the Virginia Piedmont, the Low Country of South Carolina, etc., and similar glossaries of the more important relic areas such as the coast of Maine, the Green Mountains, the Eastern Shore of Maryland, Albemarle Sound, the Alleghenies and the Appalachians. The *Linguistic Atlas* will be an effective guide in choosing the vantage points, and the word lists already published by the Dialect Society and by *American Speech* as well as the vocabulary items in the *Atlas* will suggest topics on which the collecting should be centered in the various sections.

We need, furthermore, complete topical glossaries for such things and activities as food and cooking, general farming, dairy farming, cotton culture, fishing, seafaring, mining, etc. A single glossary for each topic from any part of the country will give us the basis for preparing the necessary questionnaires for the systematic collecting that must follow.

The preparation of regional and topical glossaries would involve little expense. It could be done to a large extent by scholars already located in different sections of the country. Intelligent informants can be easily secured, as the experience of the *Atlas* staff shows. There should, of course, be a guiding spirit for all such activity.

The regional and topical glossaries would provide the basis for planning systematic collecting in a larger number of points by means of questionnaires. When this stage has been reached, say in ten years, a central repository and planning agency would have to be set up in some university.

The writer of this preface is convinced that not much progress can be made along the road we have been traveling in the last 50 years in our attempts to lay the foundation for an American dialect dictionary. With few exceptions the published word lists are too scanty to be of much use. Whole sections of the country, e.g. Pennsylvania and the entire Southern Seaboard, are unexplored. The unevenness of the available material, in a geographical sense, is brought home by Mrs. Nixon's careful compilation in which many references to the Appalachians, the Ohio Valley, the Ozarks, and New England will be found but very few to the Southern Seaboard and the Gulf States where many of the words she presents are widely current. One therefore hopes that the Dialect Society may take a new perspective and steer the work of its members into more productive channels.

October　　　　　　　　　　　　　HANS KURATH
1945　　　　　　　　　　　　　*Brown University*

INTRODUCTION

This word list presents a sampling of the Virginia vocabulary with a description of the regional and the social spread of each term in Virginia and, as far as available dictionaries and word lists permit, in the rest of the United States and in the British Isles.

These terms are taken from the 138 Virginia field records of the *Linguistic Atlas*. For each term the geographic and the social spread in Virginia is described on the basis of the findings of the *Atlas*. Some of the expressions presented here occur in all parts of Virginia, others only on the Eastern Shore, the Tidewater, the Piedmont or the Valley, or in a combination of these sections. Some are used by speakers of all social classes, others only by the common folk or the cultured. Some expressions have general currency, others are rare. The list contains primarily regional and local words, but whenever a national or a literary synonym is current in Virginia by the side of the regional or local expression, it has been included to give a complete picture of Virginia usage. To omit such terms would be to give a false view of the actual situation.

It was planned originally to use the *Atlas* records to describe the occurrence of each term in all of the Eastern States, but since these records have been edited only in part, such statements cannot be made at present.

Each term was then looked up in the following sources, which are cited always in this order and with these abbreviations: B. W. Green's *Word-Book of Virginia Folk-Speech* (VWB), *Dialect Notes* (DN), *American Speech* (AS), the *Dictionary of American English* (DAE), Richard Thornton's *American Glossary* (T), the *New English Dictionary* (NED), the *Century Dictionary* (CD), and the *English Dialect Dictionary* (EDD).

Green's *Word-Book* is quoted first. This regional glossary is very good for the Piedmont, less so for the Valley, the Tidewater, and the Eastern Shore. It does not attempt to describe the geographic spread of the terms within Virginia.

Next come the references to the word lists from different parts of the country published in *Dialect Notes* and in *American Speech*. Items from the South are given first, then those from the Midland, finally those from the North. Because of the haphazard nature of these word lists the actual geographic spread of the terms in the United States cannot yet be determined.

7

References to the dictionaries are presented last, in the order given above. Definitions are quoted from these dictionaries when they are at variance with the meanings of the Virginia terms or when they contribute something specific. Whenever a term is assigned to a particular area, the proper notation has been made. Dates of the earliest and the latest quotations have been reproduced. Words which are not included in the *Dictionary of American English* have been starred.

The treatment of the terms presented here is as full as available published sources permit, but the picture is obviously incomplete.

PHYLLIS J. NIXON

A GLOSSARY OF VIRGINIA WORDS

*abate (see *calm down, lay, lower down, moderate, moderate down*):
Of the wind, subside; rare. NED (II.14) 1400–; CD (II.1).

aim (see *be fixing*): Intend; not common. VWB. Reported
from eAla (DN 3), wcWVa (AS 2.347), wNC Mts (DN 4), Tenn
Mts (DN 1), Cumberlands (AS 7.90), Ind (AS 16.22), wInd
(DN 3), sIll (DN 2), seMo (DN 2), swMo (DN 5), nwArk (DN
2), Me (AS 2.82; DN 5, *obsolete*). DAE Now chiefly *colloq.* or
dial., 1650–1908; NEDS (5.b) *Dial.* and *U.S.*, 1665–1909; CD
(II.2); EDD: Cum, Wm, Yks, Lan, Der, War, Wor, Hrf, Glo,
Dor, Som, Dev.

alter (see *change, cut*): Castrate; fairly common. VWB.
Reported from eAla (DN 3), La (DN 1), swMo (DN 5), wNY
(DN 3), cConn (DN 3). DAE *American*; NEDS (1.b) *U.S.*
and *Austral.*, 1889–1895; CD (3) *U.S.*

angleworm (see *earthworm, fishing worm, ground worm, red
worm*): Earthworm; on the Northern Neck. Reported from Mo
(DN 3), cNY (DN 3), NE (AS 8.12), wConn (DN 1), Vt (DN
3). DAE *American*, 1832–1918; CD.

andirons (see *fire dogs, dog irons, fire irons, hand irons*): Iron
utensils used to support the wood in a fireplace; common. VWB.
DAE 1640–1891; NED 1300–1878; CD; EDD: Yks, Lan; in dial.
pron. *endirons.*

ash cake (see *ash pone*): A cornmeal cake baked in the ashes;
common everywhere. VWB A loaf of cornbread baked in the
ashes. Reported from eAla (DN 3, *rare except in reminiscences*),
seMo (DN 2), nwArk (DN 3). DAE *American* 1809–1904;
T 1839–1861; NED (8.b); NEDS *U.S.*, 1824–1887; CD.

ash pone (see *ash cake*): A cornmeal cake baked in the ashes;
fairly common. DAE *American*, 1816–1840.

ashy (see *touchous, wrathy*): Angry; not common. VWB.
Reported from Va (DN 4), Ill (DN 5), sIll (DN 2), seMo (DN
2), Mo (DN 5), nwArk (DN 3). DAE *American, colloq.*, 1846–
1903.

attic (see *garret*): The top story of a house; used mostly by the
better educated. DAE 1841–1907; NED (3) The highest storey
of a house, or a room in it, 1817–1870; CD (2).

back a letter: Address a letter; common. VWB. Reported
from Va (DN 4), eAla (DN 3), wFla (DN 1), wcWVa (AS 2.347),

wNC mts (DN 4), SC (AS 18.66), Ky (DN 4), Ind (AS 16.21), Ill (DN 1), sIll (DN 2, DN 3), neIa (DN 1), seMo (DN 2), nwArk (DN 3), Ozarks (DN 5), Kan (DN 4), Neb (DN 4), Neb Pioneer English (AS 8.51), wNY (DN 3), Me (AS 5.124). DAE (3) 1829–1902; T; NEDS (12.b) *U.S.*, 1859–1902, *So. and West;* CD; EDD: Sc.

back-house (see *garden house, johnny house*): A privy; common. VWB. Reported from eAla (DN 3, also *backy*), wNY (DN 3), cConn (DN 3), Me (DN 5, *obsolete*). DAE (b) *American*, quotations from Webster 1847, and Bartlett 1859; CD A building behind or back from the main or front building; hence, in country places, especially in New England, a privy.

ballet (see *song ballad*).

bank-barn: A barn erected on sloping ground, with three sides of the bottom story enclosed by earth; not common; in northern part of the Blue Ridge. Reported from the English of the Pa Germans (As 10.171), neO (DN 2). DAE *American*, 1894–1903; NEDS *U.S.*, 1894–1909.

barn lot, stable lot, lot: Barnyard; common everywhere except in the Shenandoah Valley and on the Eastern Shore. Reported from sIll (DN 2), nwArk (DN 3), wConn (DN 1). DAE; T A piece of land; NED (6a) ... any piece of land set apart for a particular purpose, *now chiefly U.S.*, 1633–.

barrow hog: A barrow; rare. DAE (2); NED (1.b), also *barrow-pig*, 1547–1693; CD Now chiefly prov. Eng.; EDD: Lan, Ken, Hmp; also *barrow-pig*.

*base-born (see *oldfields colt, woods colt*): Illegitimate child; on Chesapeake Bay; NED (3) 1645–1851; CD (a); EDD, *base-child*, one base born.

bateau: A flat-bottomed boat; in the Tidewater area and on the Eastern Shore. VWB A flat, light-draught boat of planks. Reported from eVa (DN 2, *by negroes*), NJ (DN 1, *by oystermen*), eMe (DN 3, *by loggers*), lumberjacks (AS 17.219, a boat used on Eastern drives), early NE words (AS 15.226). DAE *American*, 1711–1902; T 1769–1870; NED A light river boat; esp. the long tapering boats with flat bottoms used by the French Canadians, 1759–1884; CD (1) A light boat for river navigation, long in proportion to its breadth, and wider in the middle than at the ends.

batter bread (see *egg bread*): Cornbread made with eggs and milk;

east of the Blue Ridge. VWB. Reported from nwArk (DN 3, a soft corn bread containing lard or butter and served with a spoon, or a thick griddle cake of flour and meal), Cornell U. (DN 2, a preparation like hominy, eaten with butter, possibly like the *egg-bread* of Tenn). DAE *American*, 1899–1904.

batter cake (see *flannel cake, griddle cake, hot-cake*): Pancake; common everywhere. VWB A thin cake of corn meal, milk, and eggs, and baked on a hot iron. DAE *American, chiefly Southern*, 1833–1897.

beholden: Under obligation; common. VWB. Reported from Ozarks (DN 5), nwArk (DN 3), Cape Cod (DN 2, DN 3). DAE *Now dial.*, 1835–1878; NED (1) 1340–1873; CD; EDD: Irel, Yks, Lan, Stf, Not, Lei, Nhp, War, Glo, Brks, eAn, Ken, Hmp, Dor, Som.

belling: Serenade after a wedding; in the northern part of the Blue Ridge and the central part of the Piedmont. Reported from O (DN 1), Neb (AS 8.22, 1870), NY (DN 1), NE (AS 8.24, *rare*). DAE *American*, 1862.

***bite** (see *piece, snack*): A lunch eaten between meals; scattered in the Tidewater area. Reported from wcWVa (AS 2.348, a cold lunch), sIll (DN 2, sometimes also a regular meal), Western Reserve (DN 4), nwArk (DN 3, sometimes also a regular meal), NH (DN 4). NED (2) ... *concr.* food to eat; chiefly in the phrase *bite and sup*, 1562–1861; CD (5) Food; victuals: as, three days without either *bite* or sup; EDD: Sc, Nhb, Dur, Cum, Wm, Yks, Lan, Stf, Lin, Hmp, Wil, Som, Dev Slang; (1) A mouthful, a small portion of food; (2) *bite and sup*, food and drink, a slight repast.

blinds, window blinds (see *curtains, shades*): Roller shades for windows; common west of the Blue Ridge. *Blinds* reported from swPa (AS 7.19), DAE 1845–1902, NED (2) 1786–; *window blinds* NED (5.a) 1730–1865, CD.

***(be) blustering up** (see *brewing up, ketchy*): Of the weather, look stormy; used among older people, rare. VWB, *blustering*, stormy. NED (II.2), *bluster*, of the wind: To blow boisterously or with stormy violence, 1530–.

***boar hog** (see *male, male hog*): Boar; in the northern Blue Ridge, rare. Reported from Va (DN 4), eAla (DN 3, *used always*).

bonny-clabber (see *clabber*): Curdled milk; scattered. Reported from eAla (DN 3), Cape Cod (DN 2, *barney-clabber*). DAE, also *bony clabber*, *bonny clapper*, 1731–1904; NED 1631–1883; CD (1); EDD, *Obs.*, Irel, Chs.

bottom, bottoms (see *bottom land*, *low grounds*, *flats*): Low land; common everywhere. VWB Low land near a river; or between two hills; a valley. Reported from Va (AS 15.157, low land formed by alluvial deposits along a stream), nwArk (DN 3, generally used of low land). DAE (1) A stretch of low-lying land, usu. along a river or other stream, now *dial.*, 1634–1907; NED (4.b) Low-lying land, a valley, a dell; an alluvial hollow, 1325–1803; CD (3); EDD, Var. dial. uses in Sc, Irel, and Eng, also colonies; (1) the lowest part of a valley; a gully, ravine; low-lying land subject to inundation. Freq. in *pl.*

bottom land (see *bottom, low grounds, flats*): Low ground; west of the Blue Ridge and on the Rappahannock. Reported from Va (AS 15.158, rich flat land on the banks of streams; a flood plain; a bottom), swMo (DN 5). DAE *American*, 1738–1890; NEDS *U.S.*, A stretch of level land beside a river; an alluvial plain forming a river bottom, 1785–1903; CD, *bottom* (3).

branch (see *creek, run*): A small stream; common everywhere. VWB a small stream of water, brook. Reported from Va (AS 15.158–9: (1) a principal tributary of a river, creek, or other stream, (2) an arm of a cove or swamp, (3) a stream smaller than a creek; a brook or run), eAla (DN 3), Md (AS 10.256–9, most familiar in the plateau), Ohio River valley (AS 9.320, a small stream), eKy (DN 3), wInd (DN 3), sIll (DN 2, a small tributary of a small stream), Cumberlands (AS 15.47), Great Smokies (AS 15.47), seMo (DN 2), swMo (DN 5), nwArk (DN 3), Ozarks (AS 15.47). DAE A tributary of a creek or river, one of the streams which unite to form a river; *American*, a small stream, 1663–1913; T a brook; NED (2.b) *U.S.*, a small stream or brook, 1825; CD (3) In the southern and some of the western United States, the general name for any stream that is not a large river or a bayou.

*break up, break (see *let out, turn out*): *Of school*, be over; mostly in the eastern Piedmont. NED (56.e) 1535–1882; CD.

breakdown (see *frolic, hoedown, shindig*): A dance; not common. VWB, A riotous dance. Reported from eAla (DN 3), southern negroes (AS 3.209), wInd (DN 3), nwArk (DN 3), cConn (DN 3). DAE *American*, (a) To dance or perform a dance in a violent, stamping manner, 1838–1873; NED (2) *U.S.*, but frequently humorously in England, 1864–1881; CD (2), A noisy, lively dance, sometimes accompanied by singing, as in the southern United States; *U.S.*

*breast: Chest; fairly common. Reported from sIll (DN 2). NED (3) *Obs.*, 1340–1766; CD (2).

breeze up (see *getting up*): *Of the wind*, rise; along the shore, and on the Eastern Shore. VWB. Reported from Cape Cod (DN 2, *to breeze up fresh*). DAE 1752–1879; NED (2) *Naut.*

*(be) brewing up (see *blustering up, ketchy*): *Of the weather*, look stormy; not common. NED (4.c) 1530–1765; CD (II.2).

buck: Ram; west of the Blue Ridge, and on the lower Rappahannock. Reported from Va (DN 4), wcWVa (AS 2.349), Western Reserve (DN 4, *ram* considered scientific), swMo (DN 5, See *male* "bull"). DAE *American*, 1812–1881; NED (1) The male of several animals; CD.

bucket: A pail; regularly, among all classes. VWB Wooden or metal vessels, usually carried by a handle over the top. Reported from the Ohio River valley (AS 9.320, *universal*), Western Reserve (DN 4, usually a wooden bucket without a bail), the South (DN 4), eAla (DN 3), sIll (DN 2), seMo (DN 2), nwArk (DN 2), Kan (DN 4, any vessel with a bail used for carrying liquids), Neb (DN 4), wNY (DN 3, a wooden pail), Cape Cod (DN 2, a wooden pail), Hampstead, NH (DN 3, a wooden pail), West Brattleboro, Vt (DN 3, a wooden vessel without a handle or bail and having flaring sides; usually deeper than it is wide). DAE (1) A vessel for holding liquids; a pail. "The term is applied in the South and West, to all kinds of pails and cans holding over a gallon" (Bartlett, 1859), 1622–1904; NED . . . The local application of the word varies greatly; in the south-east of England and in the U. S. a bucket is a round wooden pail with an arched handle; in the south of Scotland it is a four-sided vessel for salt, coal, ashes, etc., 1300–1852; CD (1) . . . a pail or open vessel of wood, leather, metal, or other material, for carrying water or other liquid; EDD Var. dial. uses in Sc, Eng, and Amer; (1) a wooden pail, quotation from Bartlett as given in DAE above.

*bundle (see *sheaf*): A sheaf of wheat; common everywhere. Reported from Western Reserve (DN 4), nwArk (DN 3), eNeb (AS 12.106, *of hay*), wNY (DN 3). CD (1) . . . a *bundle* of hay; EDD Var. dial. uses in Sc, Eng, and Amer.

*burlap bag (see *crocus bag, grass sack, guano sack, sack bag,* *tow sack*): A large bag made of coarse canvas; not common except along the Potomac.   NED, *burlap* 1695–1880.

*buss (see *smouch*): To kiss; fairly common.   Reported from eAla (DN 3, *not common*), English of the Pa Germans (AS 10.172), Tenn Mts (DN 1, *bussy*, sweetheart, *also* AS 14.89), App Mts (DN 5, also *bussy*), Ozarks (DN 5, *not common*, perhaps by former Tenn people), Ozarks (AS 5.424).   NED *Arch.* and *dial.*, 1571–1866; CD (II); EDD: Sc, Nhb, Cum, Yks, Lan, Chs, Stf, Der, Lin, Lei, Nhp War, Shr, eAn, Ken, Sus, Hmp, Dor, Cor.

butterbeans (see *lima beans*): Lima beans; common everywhere. DAE *American*, 1841–1911; NEDS 1884–1906; CD *U.S.*

*calm down (see *abate, lay, lower, moderate, moderate down*): *Of the wind;* not common.   NED (1); CD (II).

carry (**someone home**): Escort (someone home); common east of the Blue Ridge.   Reported from Va (DN 1, DN 4, lead, ride, drive), swVa (AS 8.23), eAla (DN 3), Miss Intelligencer (DN 4, to lead a quadruped), La (DN 1), wcWVa (AS 2.350), Md (DN 1), NC (DN 5), NC Mts (DN 4, AS 8.23), Ky (DN 1), Cumberlands (AS 7.90), seArk (AS 13.5), nwArk (DN 2, DN 3), Me (DN 4, to lead).   DAE *Southern and dial.*, 1622–1896; NED (5) *arch.* and *dial.*, 1513–1886; CD (3); EDD: Ir, wCrk, Cum, wYks.

*catty-bias (see *catty-cornered, catty-wampered, cattawampus*): In a diagonal position; not common.   Reported from wKy (DN 1).

catty-cornered (see *catty-bias, catty-wampered, cattawampus*): In a diagonal position; common.   VWB.   Reported from eAla (DN 3), nwArk (DN 3), Neb (DN 3), NY (DN 1), wNY (DN 3). DAE *American*, 1837–1875; T; NED *dial.*, 1878–1881; EDD: wYks, Der, Not, Bdf, neLan, Lei, War, Shr, sChs; U.S.A.

*catty-wampered (**cattawampus**) (see *catty-bias, catty-cornered*): In a diagonal position, or awry; not common.   Reported from SC (AS 18.66, out of order), eAla (DN 3), NC Mts (DN 4), Ky (DN 4), Ind (AS 16.21), sInd (AS 14.266, DN 3), wInd (DN 3), Ill (DN 4), sIll (DN 2), seMo (DN 2), nwArk (DN 3), Kan (DN 4, awry), Neb (DN 3), NE (DN 4).

chamber (see *front room, living room, parlor, room, sitting room*): A sitting room on the first floor, usually with a bed; in the Tidewater area, among older people.   DAE 1863–1902, *Southern*; NED (I.1) . . . in some English dialects, the "parlour" or better room as distinguished from the kitchen; EDD (3) A bedroom on the ground floor: Chs, Shr.

*change (see *alter*, *cut*): Castrate; fairly common. Reported from Va (DN 4).

chittlins: Hogs' intestines; in general use east of the Blue Ridge. VWB, Hog's intestines prepared for food, linked into knots and boiled, then put into vinegar. Reported from eAla (DN 3, *also chitlin-bread*), nwArk (DN 3), Ozarks (AS 5.17). DAE *chitlings, chetlins*, etc., (1) 1880–1909; NED *chitling* (1) Another form of *chitterling*; widely used in Eng. *dial.* and in *U.S.*, 1886–1888; CD *chitterling* (1) . . . part of the frill-like small intestine, as of swine, fried for food; also a kind of sausage; EDD *chitterlings*, Sc and gen. dial. use in Eng.

Christmas gift!: Merry Christmas!, a greeting used on Christmas morning; the person who says it first receives a gift; common everywhere. Reported from Va (DN 4), eAla (DN 3), seMo (DN 2), nwArk (DN 3, used by the negroes and lower whites, a kind of begging formula). DAE *American*, 1844–1908.

clabber (see *bonny-clabber*): Curdled milk; common everywhere. VWB, also *clobber*. Reported from sIll (DN 2), nwArk (DN 3). DAE 1828 (Webster)—1894; T, otherwise *bonny-clabber, Sc;* NED (2) 1624–1884; CD; EDD (2) Mun.

*clabber cheese (see *cottage cheese, curd, home-made cheese, smear-case*): Cheese made of the drained curd of sour milk; not common; in the Blue Ridge, the northern Piedmont, and the Southern Neck. Reported from nwArk (DN 2).

*clean (across) (see *clear across, jam across, plum across*): Entirely (across); fairly common east of the Blue Ridge. VWB. Reported from Ky (DN 5), Cumberlands (AS 7.90). NED (5) *Obs.*; EDD (13) Sc, Irel, Eng.

clear (across) (see *clean across, jam across, plum across*): Entirely (across); common in the western Piedmont and the Blue Ridge. Reported from eAla (DN 3), Western Reserve and Ind (*clear done*), seMo (DN 2), nwArk (DN 3). DAE *clear through*, 1842–1901; NED (5).

clever: Good-natured; common. VWB. Reported from Va (DN 4, generous), NC (DN 4), Ky (DN 4), eKy (DN 3), sInd (DN 3, AS 14.263), Miss (DN 4), Ozarks (DN 5, AS 4.204, AS 5.425), nwArk (DN 2), Neb (DN 4), Mass (DN 2, of horses), cConn (DN 3), NH (DN 2, of horses; DN 3, of animals, and of persons who are good-natured and perhaps a little deficient mentally), Me (AS 3.140); DN 4, of oxen), Dunglison's Glossary

(DN 5.)   DAE (1) Of horses, etc. well made; (2) good-natured
. . . *colloq.*, 1758–1904; (3) honest, conscientious . . . *colloq.*, 1804–
1818; T 1768–1850; NED (III.c) *U.S. colloq.*, 1773–1846; CD
(4) *colloq. U.S.;* EDD: Gall, Hr, eAn, Hrf, Suf, Cor.

coal hod (see *scuttle*): Along the Potomac; not common. Reported from NY (DN 1,—In the stove and hardware trade *coal
hod* is universal, and this form is more common in cities; in the
usage of country families in central N.Y. *coal scuttle* seems to
predominate.), cConn (DN 3).   DAE 1848–1895; CD.

coal oil (see *lamp oil*): Kerosene oil; common between the
Potomac and the Rappahannock, and in the Shenandoah Valley,
scattered elsewhere.   Reported from New Orleans, La (DN 4),
language of the oil wells (DN 2), Pa (DN 4), O (DN 1), Ill (DN
1), nwArk (DN 5), Neb (DN 4), Neb pioneer English (AS 7.167),
English Canada (DN 1).   DAE *American*, petroleum or oil
refined from it, especially kerosene, 1858–1908; NED *U.S.*, Shale-
oil, petroleum, 1858–1926; CD.

comfort: A thick bed quilt; regularly everywhere. VWB.
Reported from eAla (DN 3).   DAE 1843–1913; NED (8) *U.S.*;
CD *comfortable* (II) A thickly wadded and quilted bedcover.
Also *comfort* and *comforter, U.S.*

corn bread (see *corn pone, pone bread*): Cornmeal bread; common everywhere. VWB. DAE *American*, 1796–1898; NED
U.S., 1823–1913; CD *U.S.*

corn cakes (see *hoe cake, johnny cake*): Cornmeal griddle cakes;
fairly common.   DAE *American*, 1791–1863; NED *U.S.*, 1850–
1854; CD *U.S.*

corn crib (see *corn house, corn stack*): West of the Blue
Ridge. VWB. Reported from nwArk (DN 3), cConn (DN 3).
DAE *American*, 1687–1908; T 1809–1849; NED *U.S.* 1849–
1883; CD.

corn dodger (see *dodger, pone*): A hard, hand-shaped cake of
cornbread; west of the Blue Ridge and in the northern parts of the
Piedmont and Tidewater. VWB A dumplin' made of corn
meal and boiled in a pot with ham and cabbage.   Reported from
eAla (DN 3), Ky (DN 1), wInd (DN 3), seMo (DN 2), nwArk
(DN 3, plain cornbread or cornbread baked in a skillet), Neb
pioneer English (AS 6.250, AS 7.168).   DAE *American*, Bread
made of Indian corn meal baked hard in small cakes or pones,
1834–1909; NED *U.S.*, 1856–1885; CD *So. U.S.*

corn house (see *corn crib, corn stack*): Corn crib; everywhere east of the Blue Ridge except south of the lower James. Reported from wNY (DN 3). DAE *American,* 1699–1891; NED (2) *U.S.*; CD *U.S.*

* **corn stack** (see *corn crib, corn house*): Corn crib; on the Eastern Shore.

corn pone (see *corn bread, pone bread*): Corn bread; common everywhere. DAE *American* and *Southern,* bread made of Indian corn meal, water or milk, and salt, usu. baked in small loaves or masses, 1859–1904; NED *So. U.S.,* 1860–1890; CD *So. U.S.*

* **corruption:** Pus; common. VWB. Reported from Va (DN 4), eAla (DN 3), sIll (DN 2), seMo (DN 2). NED *Obs.* exc. *dial.,* 1526–1888; CD (2); EDD: NI, nYks, Chs, nLin.

cottage cheese (see *clabber cheese, curd, home-made cheese, smear case*): Cheese made of the drained curd of sour milk; regarded as a modern term. DAE *American* 1848 (Bartlett)— 1917; CD *U.S.,* also called *Dutch cheese, pot cheese, smear case.*

counterpane (see *coverlid*): A bedspread; common. VWB. Reported from wcWVa (AS 2.352), NC Mts (DN 4), Ky (DN 4). DAE 1687–1900; NED A coverlet, a quilt 1464–1885; CD ... a quilt; now, *spec.,* a coverlet woven of cotton with raised figures, also called Marseilles quilt.

coverlid (see *counterpane*): A bedspread; rare. VWB A cover for a bed, bed quilt, coverled. DAE 1640–1913; NED 1300–1862; CD; EDD: eYks, Chs, nLin, Nhp, War, Hnt, Ken.

cow pen (see *cow pound, cuppen, milk gap*): Pen for cows; common. DAE 1661–1904; NED 1635–1876.

cow pound (see *cow pen, cuppen, milk gap*): Pen for cows; on the Eastern Shore and on the point of land east of Norfolk. VWB *pound* A farm pen. DAE *pound* An enclosure built and maintained at public expense for impounding stray or trespassing stock, 1633–1902; NED *pound* (I.1.c) An enclosure for sheltering or in any way dealing with sheep or cattle in the aggregate, 1780–1890; CD *See* DAE; EDD *pound* (1) A small enclosure; a sheepfold; a pig-sty: Sh I, Yks, Stf, War, Shr, Hrf, Glo, Sur, Sus, Hmp, Som, Dev, and Amer.

creek (see *branch, run*): A fresh water stream, common everywhere; a narrow salt water inlet, on the Tidewater and Eastern Shore. VWB a small stream where there is an ebb and flow of the tide. Reported from Va (AS 15.168: (1) in the lower Tidewater an arm of the sea . . . also a stream opening into a large river and subject to the tide, (2) a fresh-water stream normally smaller than a river and larger than a brook in the same general locality; usually distinguished from river and branch), SC (DN 4), Pa (DN 4), Md (AS 10.256–9, most frequent in the coastal plain), Western Reserve (DN 4), Mo (DN 1), nwArk (DN 3), Kan (DN 4), Neb (DN 4), Cal (DN 5), wNY (DN 3), NY (DN 4), Aroostook, Me (DN 3); Dunglison's Glossary (DN 5,—a small river, southern and middle states; "In New England it has the correct English signification; a part of a sea, lake, or river running into the land."). DAE (1) an inlet of the ocean or of a river, common in New England records of the 17th century and still in local use; (2) *American*, a stream forming a tributary to a larger river: a small stream, brook, or rivulet, 1638–1843; T A small river, 1674–1869; NED (I.1) A narrow recess or inlet in the coastline of the sea, or the tidal estuary of a river; (2.b) in *U.S.* and *Brit. Colonies*, a a branch of a main river, a tributary river; a rivulet, brook, small stream, or run, 1674–1848; CD (1) A small inlet . . . ; (2) A small stream; a brook; a rivulet; common in this sense in the United States and Australia, but now rare in England.

crocus bag, crocus sack, croker sack (see *burlap bag, grass-sack, guano sack, sack, sack bag, tow sack*): A large bag made of coarse canvas; common in the southern Piedmont, scattered in the northern Piedmont. Reported from eAla (DN 3, coker-sack), wFla (DN 1). DAE *crocus, American*, a kind of coarse, heavy cloth, *Obs.*, 1689–1790; NED (5) *crocus ginger-bagg* 1699.

cuppen, cow-cuppen (see *cow pen, cow pound, milk gap*): A pen for cows; the Piedmont and the Northern Neck. VWB (2) An enclosure in which animals are kept. DAE *American, Southern*, 1823–1899; NED (I.1.c) An enclosure for sheltering or in any way dealing with sheep or cattle in the aggregate, 1780–1890; EDD: Sh, Yks, Stf, War, Shr, Hrf, Glo, Sur, Sus, Hmp, Som, Dev, and Australia, (1) A small enclosure; a sheepfold; a pig-sty.

cur-dog (see *fiste*): A mongrel dog; common. VWB A cur, worthless dog, of unknown breed and blood but mean stock. Reported from sInd (DN 3), sIll (DN 2), nwArk (DN 3). DAE 1791–1885; NED (1.c) 1225–1859; CD; EDD (2) A collie or shepherd's dog, Cum.

curds, curd cheese (see *clabber cheese, cottage cheese, home-made* *cheese, smear-case*): Cheese made of the drained curd of sour milk, especially that fed to turkeys or chickens; mostly in the Tidewater area. DAE; CD (1).

curtains (see *blinds, shades*): Roller shades for windows; common in the Tidewater and the eastern Piedmont. Reported from nwArk (DN 3), seIa (DN 2), wNY (DN 3), Me (DN 5, AS 2.79). DAE (1) 1640–1902; NED (1) 1300–1827.

* cut (see *alter, change*): Castrate; common. VWB. Reported from wcWVa (AS 2.351), Western Reserve (DN 4), eNeb (AS 12.104), Cal (DN 5, *common at U. of Cal.*). NED (26.a) 1465–1865; CD (9); EDD (4) wYks, Chs, nLin, swLin, sWor, Shr, Ess, wSom.

dike up (see *fix up, primp up, prink*): Get dressed up; fairly common. VWB. Reported from Va (DN 4, *dike*, n and vb), Charlottesville, Va (DN 2), Wedgefield, SC (DN 6), eAla (DN 3), wTex (DN 4), Tex (DN 1), wcWVa (AS 2.352), nwArk (DN 3), NJ (DN 1, *dicked, on a dike*, showing one's finery in public). DAE *American* 1851–1923; NEDS s. and vb., *U.S. slang* or *colloq.*, 1871–1923.

dip: A pudding sauce; not common. Reported from NJ (DN 1), eKy (DN 3, cream for coffee), nwArk (DN 3), Ozarks (DN 5, sweetened cream, eaten with pie, apple dumpling, cobbler, and the like), ranch diction of the Texas panhandle (AS 8.27). DAE (3) A sauce or dressing, *local*, 1846–1894; NED (9) *local Eng. and U.S.*, 1825–1884; CD (5.b) *local, U.S.*; EDD (10): nCy, cYks, wYks, Chs, nwDer, Lei, Nhp, War, Hnt, eAn, Nrf, Amer; also *brandy-dip*.

dirt-daubers (see *masons, mud-daubers*): Wasps; common. Reported from Va (DN 4), eAla (DN 3), Ozarks (AS 8.48). DAE *American* and *Southern*, a sand-wasp or mud-dauber, 1844–1902; NED (2) A species of sand-wasp.

disremember: Not remember; common. VWB. Reported from south (DN 1, *common, though considered vulgar*), eAla (DN 3, *common*), Miss (DN 4), wTex (DN 4, *widely used*), wInd (DN 3), sIll (DN 2), nwArk (DN 3, *rare*), Ozarks (AS 5.425), Sherwood's Provincialisms (DN 5), Dunglison's Glossary (DN 5). DAE chiefly *dial.*, 1815–1917; T *dial.* in England and common in the north of Ireland; NED Chiefly *dial.*, 1836–1880; CD *Vulgar*; EDD: Sc, Irel, Lan, Lin, Oxf. Brks, Sus, Hmp, Corn, Amer.

dodger (see *corn dodger, pone*): A hard, hand-shaped cake of cornbread; west of the Blue Ridge and in the northern Piedmont and Tidewater. Reported from eAla (DN 3), Ky (DN 1), seMo (DN 2), nwArk (DN 3). DAE *American*, 1831–1894; T A soft cake of wheat or maize, somewhat resembling a pancake, 1834–1864; NED (2) *U.S.*, a hard-baked corn-cake, 1852–1882; CD (3) *U.S.*

dog irons (see *andirons, fire dogs, fire irons, hand irons*): Iron utensils used to support the wood in a fireplace; common from the Blue Ridge westward, and south of the lower James—less common in the Piedmont. Reported from swMo (DN 5), Ozarks (AS 8.48), Newfoundland (DN 5). DAE 1790–1884; NED 1883; EDD See *fire dogs*.

* **doney:** Girl friend; not common. Reported from NC Mts (DN 4, AS 15.46, also *doney-gal*), Ky Mts (DN 5, usually *doney-gal*). NED *Doña* (2) *Slang*, 1873–1894.

* **dry-land frog** (see *hop-toad, toad-frog*): A toad; common.

earthworm (see *angleworm, fishing worm, ground worm, red-worm*): On the lower James. Reported from NE (AS 8.12, *general and literary term*). DAE 1737–1883; NED (1); CD (1).

egg bread (see *batter bread*): A soft bread made of corn meal and eggs; mostly south of the lower James and in the northern Piedmont. Reported from sMiss (DN 2), Tenn (DN 2). DAE *American*, 1854–1904; T 1862; NEDS (7) *U.S.*, 1862.

evening: Afternoon, from noon until sunset; common. Reported from eAla (DN 3), Barbourville, Ky (DN 3), wInd (DN 3), sIll (DN 2), seMo (DN 2), swMo (DN 5), Ozarks (AS 8.48), nwArk (DN 2), Newfoundland (DN 5), Dunglison's Glossary, labeled "southern states" (DN 5). DAE (2) *S. & W., dial.*, 1790–1904; NEDS (2.c) *dial.* and *U.S. local*, 1836–1888; CD (3) England and so. U.S.; EDD (1) Wor, Shr, Sur.

fair up: Of weather, to clear; used among older people, not common. VWB. Reported from Shenandoah Valley (AS 12.287) eAla (DN 3), Ozarks (AS 8.49), Vt (DN 5, *fair off*). DAE *dial.*, 1859–; NED (1.b) *rare exc. dial.*, 1842–1891; CD (II.2) *fair* . . . followed commonly by *up* or *off* (Scotch); EDD (16) Cai, Nhb, eDur, nYks, neYks, wYks, Amer (Bartlett).

falling weather: Bad weather, rain; not common. Reported from Lynchburg, Va (DN 4), NC (DN 4), wVa (DN 4), wcWVa (AS 2.353), sInd (DN 3), sIll (DN 2), seMo (DN 1), seArk (AS 13.5), nwArk (DN 3), Ozarks (AS 8.49), Kan (DN 4). DAE *American* 1732–1919; EDD (7) War, sWor, Hrf, Glo.

*favor (someone): Resemble (someone); common. VWB. Reported from eAla (DN 3, *universal*), wcWVa (AS 2.354), Springdale, Pa (DN 1), Tenn Mts (DN 1), seMo (DN 2), swMo (DN 5), nwArk (DN 3, *the favor to you*), nNH (DN 4), Me (AS 5.127), Me rural (DN 4). T; NED (8) *now colloq.* 1609–1866; CD *now chiefly colloq.*; EDD Sc, Eng, Amer.

fire dogs, dogs (see *andirons, dog irons, fire irons, hand irons*): Iron utensils used to support the wood in a fireplace; in the southern part of the Blue Ridge and all of the Piedmont. VWB. Reported from seMo (DN 2), nwArk (DN 3), Ozarks (AS 8.48). DAE *fire dogs*, 1792–1905, *dogs* (2.a) 1641–1884; T *fire dogs* 1792–1840; NED *fire dogs* 1840, *dogs* (8) 1596–1862; CD; EDD *dogs* (10) . . . also in comp., *dog-irons:* nCy, Dur, Nhp, War, Brks, eAn, Sus, Hmp, Dor, wSom.

fire irons (see *andirons, dog irons, fire dogs, hand irons*): Iron utensils used to support the wood in a fireplace; not common. DAE Implements, usually made of iron, for use about a domestic fire; also, andirons, 1648–1885.

fishing worm, fish worm (see *angleworm, earthworm, ground worm, red worm*): Earthworm; common everywhere except on Chesapeake Bay. Reported from eAla (DN 3), nwArk (DN 3), NE (AS 8.12). DAE *American* 1870–1913; CD.

fiste (see *cur-dog*): A mongrel dog; scattered everywhere. VWB A small worthless dog. Reported from eAla (DN 3, *faust, faust-dog, fausty, fice, fice-dog*), NC Mts (DN 4, *feist, feisty*), Ky (DN 1), Tenn Mts (DN 1, also *fisty*, low or mean), sIll (DN 2, an under-sized, vicious dog), Shurtleff College, Ill (AS 3.217, *fisty*, peevish, teasing, of persons), seMo (AS 17.248, *fiesty person*, an uppish person; DN 2, *fist*, cur), nwArk (DN 3),ʼ Okla (AS 18.111, A *feisty person*, a willful person), Kan (DN 4, *feisty*, worthless; AS 17.248, cowardly), eNeb (AS 12.103, *fyst*, a bad-tempered horse), Wisc (AS 18.111, *fees*, repugnant). DAE *American*, 1805–1886; T *So.*; NED (2) *U.S. dial.*, 1872; CD (Quotation from Trans. Amer. Phil. Ass. XVIII): "*Fice* is the name used everywhere in the South, and in some parts of the West, for a small worthless cur."

(be) fixing to (see *aim to*): Plan or intend to; common. Reported from Va (DN 4), eAla (DN 3), New Orleans, La (DN 4), NC (DN 4), Ill (DN 4), nwArk (DN 2), Kan (DN 4), Sherwood's Provincialisms (DN 5), Dunglison's Glossary (DN 5). DAE *colloq.*, 1716–1914; NEDS (16.a) *U.S.* 1716–1904.

fix up (see *dike up, primp up, prink*): Get dressed up; fairly common. VWB. Reported from Ozarks (AS 11.315, *fixy*, well-groomed). DAE *American* 1834–1871; NEDS (16.b) To put oneself in proper trim; to spruce up, *U.S.*; CD (b) *colloq.*, *U.S.*

flannel cake (see *batter cake, griddle cake, hot-cake*): A pancake; mostly west of the Blue Ridge, also on Chesapeake Bay. DAE 1847–1916; T A soft thin cake usually eaten with molasses; NED (6.c) 1792; CD A kind of thin griddle-cake made with either wheat-flour or corn-meal and raised with yeast, *U.S.*; EDD (3) A coarse oatcake, wYks.

flats (see *bottom, bottom land, low-grounds*): Low level land; common in the Piedmont and on the Northern Neck. VWB A shoal or sand bank, a part of the shore uncovered at low tide. Reported from Va (AS 15.178: (1) a piece of level ground, (2) a level tract lying at a little depth below the surface of the water or alternately covered and left bare by the tide), wNY (DN 3), cConn (DN 3). DAE Low land, valuable as pasture or farm land, 1651–1829; NED (5) A piece of level ground . . . the low ground through which a river flows, 1296–1877; CD (2) . . . in the United States, a low alluvial plain near the tide-water or along a river, as the Jersey . . . flats; also the part of a shore that is uncovered at low tide; EDD (5) A hollow in a field; a small valley: neLan, Glo, Sus; Glo smaller than a *bottom*.

foreigner: A stranger, or a person from another state; fairly common. Reported from So App Mts (AS 15.46 *furrin*, anything strange), seMo (DN 2), Ozarks (AS 4.203, AS 15.46 *furrin*, anything strange), nwArk (DN 3). DAE . . . a non-native, an outsider, 1626–1886; NED (2) Now *dial.*, 1460–1875; CD (2) One who does not belong to a certain class, association, society, etc., an outsider; EDD Gen. *dial.* use in Sc, Irel, Eng, Amer.

(be) fresh, (come) fresh (see *freshen, hommy*): Calve; common. Reported from Va (DN 4), swMo (DN 5). DAE (2) 1884–1896; NEDS (10.c) *U.S.*, 1884–1896.

*freshen (see *fresh, hommy*): Calve; common. Reported from wcWVa (AS 2.354), swMo (DN 5), eMe (DN 3). NED (1.d) *U.S.*, 1931; EDD: wYks, nwDer.

*frogstool: Toadstool; not common. VWB. Reported from eAla (DN 3), Tenn Mts (DN 1), nwArk (DN 3). NED (8.b) 1661–1865; CD; EDD: Glo, sWil.

frolic (see *breakdown, hoedown, shindig*): A party; fairly common. VWB. Reported from eAla (DN 3, a country dance), seMo (DN 2, a country dance), Humphrey's Glossary (DN 5, country festival sports); DAE (1) 1711–1898; T 1767–1854; NED (2) 1645–1895; CD (2); EDD eAn, Any kind of entertainment or outing; not necessarily with the idea of amusement.

front room (see *chamber, living room, parlor, room, sitting room*): A living room'; in the James Valley and southward.—Reported from swMo (DN 5), eNeb (AS 12.102), Me (AS 5.127). DAE 1679–.

galluses (gallowses): Suspenders; common. VWB. Reported from eAla (DN 3), wcWVa (AS 2.355), Ky (DN 1), sIll (DN 2), nwArk (DN 3, s and vb), swMo (DN 5), wNY (DN 3, *less common than formerly*), NY (DN 1, to *gallows up* one's breeches), Cape Cod (DN 2), West Brattleboro, Vt (DN 3), nNH (DN 4), Me (DN 4, DN 5, AS 5.120), Aroostook, Me (DN 3), Newfoundland (DN 5), New Brunswick (DN 1, to *slip one's gallows*, lose a button). DAE *gallows, colloq.*, usu. *pl.*, 1806–1891; *gallus dial.*, usu. *pl.*, 1835–1888; T 1806–1867; NED (6) Now *dial.*, *Sc* and *U.S.*, in form *gallowses*, whence occas. *gallows* for a single brace; CD (I) *pl.*, *colloq.*; EDD (6): Sc, Bnff, Frf, eFif, Lnk, Edb, Gall, Ir, NI, sDon, sIr, Nhb, Dur, Cum, Yks, Lan, Chs, Der, nLin, Nrf, Suf, IW, Wil, nDev, (Amer., slip one's gallows "lose a button," DN 1).

* **garden house** (see *back-house, johnny house*): A privy; common everywhere except the southern part of the Piedmont. VWB. NED (1.b) *dial.* and *U.S.*; EDD (2) wSom "the usual name amongst farmers' wives and women of the class above labourers."

garret (see *attic*): The top story of a house; common. Reported from Cape Cod (DN 2), Me (AS 2.79). DAE 1637–1890; NED (2) A room on the uppermost floor of a house; an apartment formed either partially or wholly within the roof, an attic, 1483–1874; CD (2); EDD (2) A half-open upper room; wYks "Not precisely the same as *attic*, which is an upper room."

* **gentleman cow** (see *male, ox, steer*): A bull; on the Middle Neck in the presence of women. Reported from wInd (DN 3, used by squeamish women). NED *gentleman* (7.b).

* **getting up** (see *breeze up*): *Of the wind*, rising; not common. NED (72.d) 1556–1890.

goobers, goober peas (see *ground peas*): Peanuts; fairly common. Reported from Va (DN 5), eAla (DN 3), Ky (DN 5), NC (DN 5), Tenn (DN 1), seMo (DN 2), swMo (DN 5), nwArk (DN 3). DAE *goober* or *gouber, American, S.* and *SW*, 1848–1904; *goober pea, American,* 1871–1901; NED *U.S.*, 1885–1888.

granny, granny-woman: Midwife; common everywhere. VWB. Reported from NC Mts (DN 4, *granny-doctor*), App Mts (DN 5), swMo (DN 5), Ozarks (DN 5). DAE *American* (1) 1794–1824; NED *U.S., local,* 1794.

* **grass sack, sea grass sack** (see *burlap bag, crocus bag, guano sack, sack, sack bag, tow sack*): A large bag made of coarse canvas; on the Rappahannock and the Potomac. CD *grass cloth* (2) A thick fabric made in the Canary islands of some vegetable fiber.

* **green-beans** (see *snaps, string beans*): String beans; west of the Blue Ridge.

griddle cake (see *batter cake, flannel cake, hot-cake*): A pancake; in the Piedmont and Tidewater among cultured people, rare. DAE 1783–; NED (4) 1783–1852; CD *U.S.*; EDD (3.2) Ir, wYks, nCy, Amer.

* **grindrock:** Grindstone; rare. Reported from NC Mts (DN 4, *grindin' rock*), Tenn Mts (DN 1).

grist (of corn) (see *turn of corn*): The amount of corn taken to (or from) the mill at one time; in the Shenandoah Valley. VWB That which is ground; corn to be ground; grain carried to the mill to be ground separately for the owner. The quantity ground at one time, the grain carried to the mill for grinding at one time. Applied to small quantities. DAE 1640–1905; T A quantity of anything, 1833–1910; NED (2) Corn which is to be ground; also (with *pl.*) a batch of such corn, 1430–1896, (3) Corn that has been ground 1566–1887; CD See VWB; EDD In *gen.* dial. and prov. use in Sc and Eng, (1) The quantity of corn sent to a mill to be ground; meal or flour after grinding; the fee paid at a mill, *gen.* in kind, for grinding.

ground peas (see *goobers*): Peanuts; common. VWB. Reported from eAla (DN 3, not as common as *goober*), seMo (DN 2), nwArk (DN 3). DAE *American,* 1769–1892; NEDS 1769–1854; CD.

ground worm (see *angleworm, earthworm, fishing worm, redworm*): An earthworm; on the Eastern Shore and on the shore of the Middle Neck. DAE *American,* cut worm, 1708–; NEDS *U.S.*, cut worm.

guano sack (see *burlap bag, crocus bag, grass sack, sack, sack bag, tow sack*): A large bag made of coarse canvas; in the northern Piedmont. CD *guana*.

gully-washer (see *squall*): A thunderstorm; not common. Reported from sInd (AS 14.263), nwMo (DN 5), Ozarks (AS 8.49). DAE 1903.

handirons (see *andirons, dog irons, fire dogs, fire irons*): Iron utensils used to support the wood in a fireplace; on the Eastern Shore, and south to the James in the Piedmont and Tidewater. DAE 1649–1836; NED *Obs.*, 1475–1731; CD.

* **hasslet** (see *pluck*): The edible inner parts of a pig or calf; in general use east of the Blue Ridge. VWB. Reported from eAla (DN 3, *haslet*, the windpipe of an animal, or the liver and lights of a slaughtered pig), Zebulon, NC (AS 17.77), Cape Cod (DN 2, *haslet*, the liver, lights, and tongue of a killed pig), nNH (DN 4), Me (DN 4). NED A piece of meat to be roasted, esp. the entrails of a hog, 13. .–1872; CD; EDD: Sc, Chs, Lin, Nhp, War, Wor, Shr, Hrf, Glo, Brks, Suf, Ken, Hup, IW, Wil; (1) the liver and lights of a pig, (2) a dish of pigs' entrails.

hay cock (see *hay doodle, shock*): A pile of hay in the field at haying time; west of the Blue Ridge, on the Middle Neck and on the Eastern Shore. Reported from eNeb (AS 12.107). DAE 1684–1904; NED 1470–1851; EDD (13) Wil.

* **hay doodle** (see *hay cock, shock*): A pile of hay in the field at haying time; in the Blue Ridge, rare. Reported from eNeb (AS 12.106, a small stack of leftover bundles of hay).

hoe cake (see *corn cake, johnny cake*): A griddle cake made of corn meal; mostly in the Tidewater and on the Rappahannock. VWB Bread of cornmeal, water and salt, baked on the bottom of an old weeding-hoe. Reported from eAla (DN 3, baked in a flat pone in an open vessel), seMo (DN 2, baked on a board or in an open vessel before the fire), nwArk (DN 3). DAE *American, chiefly Southern;* also a similar cake of wheat, 1774–1916; T A flat cake formerly baked on a hoe over coals, 1787–1857; NED *U.S.*, 1793–1885; CD Coarse bread, generally in the form of a thin cake, made of Indian meal, water, and salt: originally that cooked on the broad, thin blade of a cottonfield hoe; *So U.S.*

hoedown (see *breakdown, frolic, shindig*): A lively dance; fairly common. Reported from wcWVa (AS 2.357), sInd (DN 3, a rough dance), wInd (DN 3, an evening of old-fashioned dancing;

more familiar than breakdown), sIll (DN 2), nwArk (DN 3, a'
rough or "lowclass" dance), Neb pioneer English (AS 8.48).
DAE *American, originally and chiefly Southern*, (1) a lively dance
1849–1898, (2) a party of such dances 1870–1887; T A negro dance
1855–1885; NED *U.S.* A noisy, riotous dance, 1860–1885; CD
Same as *breakdown*, *So U.S.*

hog's head cheese (see *pudding, souse*): A sausage of pig's
entrails; fairly common. DAE *American*, 1859 (Bartlett)–1870.

* **home-made cheese** (see *clabber cheese, cottage cheese, curd,
smear case*): Cheese made of the drained curd of sour milk; in
the Shenandoah Valley, uncommon.

* **(have a) hommy, (find a) hommy** (see *fresh, freshen*): Calve;
in the northern Blue Ridge, rare. Reported in the English of the
Pa Germans (AS 10.169).

hoppergrass: Grasshopper; in the eastern Piedmont and the
Tidewater. VWB. Reported from eAla (DN 3), So App Mts
(AS 15.53), seMo (DN 2), Ozarks (AS 15.53), wTex (DN 3),
Neb (DN 3, *facetious*), Cape Cod (DN 2, a troublesome woman
or child), Dunglison's Glossary (DN 5, "often used in the South
. . . a *vulgarism*"), Americanisms of a Hundred Years Ago (AS
7.96). DAE *American, colloq.*, 1829–1899.

hop-toad (see *dry-land frog, toad frog*): A toad; common.
Reported from sInd (DN 3, *common*), sIll (DN 2), nwArk (DN
3), Neb (DN 3, *common*). DAE *American, colloq.*, 1827–1906;
T 1827–1861; NEDS *Local U.S.*, 1827–1913.

hot-cake (see *batter cake, flannel-cake, griddle cake*): A pancake; on the Eastern shore, rare. Reported as a westernism (AS
1.150). DAE (1) 1683–1835.

* **hunkers (hunkles):** Haunches; fairly common. Reported
from So App Mts (AS 15.46, *hunker down*, to squat), SC (AS
18.67), Tenn (DN 4), Erie Canal (AS 6.98, *hunkered*), sInd (DN
3, knees), Ind (AS 16.23), swMo (DN 5, *hunker down*), Ozarks
(AS 8.50 and AS 15.46 *hunker down*), nwArk (DN 3, *usually of
animals*), Kan (DN 4), wTex (DN 4). NED 1785–1898; CD
Scotch; EDD: Sc, Irel, nCy, Nhb, Dur, Cum, Yks, Suf; Amer.

* **Irish potatoes:** White potatoes; fairly common. VWB.
Reported from Va (DN 4), NC (DN 4), Tenn (DN 4), Ill (DN 4),
New Orleans, La (DN 4), Iowa (DN 4).

jacket (see *weskit*): A vest; fairly common among older people
in the southern part of the Blue Ridge. VWB A short coat or

body garment; any garment for the body coming not lower than the hips. DAE (2) *Obs.*, 1705–1738; NED (1.d) *locally* in *U.S.*; CD (3) *local*, *U.S.*; EDD (2) Nhb, Dur.

jam (across) (see *clean across, clear across, plum across*): Entirely (across); on the Middle Neck. Reported from eAla (DN 3), nwArk (DN 3). DAE *American*, 1882–; NED (2) 1835–1921; EDD *jam full*.

johnny cake (see *corn cake, hoe cake*): A corn meal griddle cake; on the Northern Neck. VWB A cake made of corn meal and water or milk and salt, baked on a board set on edge before the fire. Reported from eAla (DN 3), Neb pioneer English (AS 7.168), cNY (DN 3), cConn (DN 3). DAE *American* (1) A flat cake of corn meal etc. cooked in various ways, on a board before the open fire, on a griddle, in a pan or oven, 1739–1903; T; NED (a) *U.S.*, a cake made of maize-meal, in the So. states toasted before a fire, elsewhere usu. baked in a pan; (b) *Austr.*, a cake made of wheat-meal, baked on the ashes or fried in a pan, 1775–1892; CD (1) In *So. U.S.* a cake of Indian meal mixed with water or milk, seasoned with salt, and baked or toasted by being spread on a board set on edge before a fire; (2) in other parts of the U.S., any unsweetened flat cake of Indian meal, sometimes mixed with mashed pumpkin (esp. in New England) and usu. baked in a pan.

* johnny house (see *back-house, garden house*): Privy; fairly common in the James Valley and the southern part of the Blue Ridge.

ketchy (see *blustering up, brewing up*): Of the weather, stormy; used among older people, rare. Reported from Ozarks (AS 11.315), NJ (DN 1, *catchy*, irritable), NY (DN 1). DAE *catching*, Variable, uncertain, unexpected, 1868–1876; NED (4) Occurring in snatches, fitful, spasmodic, 1872–; *catchy wind* 1883.

kick (see *mitten, sack*): Jilt (someone); common. VWB. Reported from eAla (DN 3). DAE *American, colloq.*, 1848; NED (4.c) *U.S. Slang*, 1860–1895; CD *Vulgar, So. U.S.*

* (no) kin (to someone): (Not) related (to someone); common among all classes. VWB. Reported from eAla (DN 3), sInd (DN 3), sIll (DN 2), seMo (DN 2), swMo (DN 5), nwArk (DN 3), Cape Cod (DN 2, not *like* someone). NED 1597–1870; CD (3); EDD: Sc, nCy, Cum, Yks, Lan, Sur, Som, Dev.

* kinfolks: Relatives; common among all classes. VWB. Reported from eAla (DN 3), Cumberlands (AS 7.93), sIll (DN

2), seMo (DN 2), swMo (DN 5), nwArk (DN 3). NED *kins-folk*, now *rare*, 1450–1855.

* **lamp oil** (see *coal oil*): Kerosene oil; in the southern parts of the Blue Ridge and the Piedmont. NED Oil used for burning in a lamp, 1581–1895.

* **(be) laying** (see *abate, calm down, lower down, moderate*): Of the wind, subside; fairly common. Reported from Ky (DN 5), sInd (DN 3), sIll (DN 2), nwArk (DN 3). EDD *lay*, sb. (26) Of waves, a temporary lull, Cai.

let out (see *break up, turn out*): *Of school*, be over; everywhere, but not common south of the James. VWB. Reported from Ind (AS 16.22 *to let out school*). DAE *American* (4.b) 1867–1898; NED (34.a) *Obs.*, 1154–1889; CD (II.c) *Rural, U.S.;* EDD (III.1.10.g) Abd.

light-bread: Wheat bread; common. VWB. Reported from Va (DN 4), eAla (DN 3), wFla (DN 1), wcWVa (AS 2.359), sIll (DN 2), seMo (DN 2), nwArk (DN 2), seKan (DN 4). DAE *American, Southern,* 1821–1920.

lighterd, lightwood: Kindling; everywhere east of the Blue Ridge. VWB Very resinous pine wood. Reported from wcWVa (AS 2.359), eAla (DN 3, *liderd*), nwLa (DN 4), Chicago people of NE antecedents (DN 3). DAE *American, Southern,* 1705–1905; T 1705–1856; NED *North Amer.* and *West Indian* (a) any wood used in lighting a fire; in the Southern states, resinous pine-wood, 1693–1888; CD . . . in the *So. U.S.*, very resinous pine wood.

lightning-bug: Firefly; common among all classes. Reported from wInd (DN 3). DAE *American* 1778–1899; T 1787–1860; NED 1806–1850; CD.

lima beans (see *butterbeans*): Considered a modern term. DAE 1822–1901; NED 1858.

living room (see *chamber, front room, parlor, room, sitting room*): Used among younger, better educated people. DAE 1857–1910; NEDS (2) *U.S.*, 1867–1911; CD.

* **load** (see *turn*): The total amount (of wood, etc.) that can be carried by a person at one time; in the Shenandoah Valley, rare. VWB A large quantity of anything. NED (2) 1225–1882; CD (1); EDD (2) A measure of weight varying according to the district and commodity.

log fence (see *rail fence, worm fence*): A rail fence; rare. DAE *American* 1651–1902.

* **lot** (see *patch*): A field (of tobacco, etc.); not common. NED (6.a) . . . any piece of land set apart for a particular purpose, *now chiefly U.S.*, 1633–.

* **lower down** (see *abate, be laying, moderate, moderate down*): Of the wind, subside; rare. NED (4.a) *lower*; CD (II) *lower.*

low-grounds (see *bottom, bottom land, flats*): Low land; common south of the Rappahannock in the Piedmont and Tidewater. VWB Meadow or bottom land. Reported from Va (AS 17.281). DAE 1659–1898; NED (IV.20) 1897.

* **lucky-bone** (see *pull bone, pully bone, wishbone*): Wishbone; east of the Blue Ridge, scattered. Reported from Cape Cod (DN 2). EDD A bone in the sheep's head worn for luck.

lumber (see *trumpery*): Junk; common everywhere. VWB. DAE 1642–1900; NED Disused articles of furniture and the like, which take up room inconveniently, or are removed to be out of the way, 1552–1884; CD (1), also *lumber-room*; EDD sb. and vb.: Sc, Wm, Yks, Lan, Chs, Not, Lin, Rut, Nhp, Shr, Oxf, Bdf, eAn, seCy, Sur.

* **male** (see *gentleman cow, ox, steer*): Bull; used everywhere, mostly in the presence of women. Reported from Va (DN 4), swMo (DN 5, any male animal kept for breeding. *Bull, boar, stallion* and *jack* are not used in mixed company, although *buck*, a male sheep or goat, and *crower*, rooster, are not considered objectionable); also *male-cow, male-brute*, etc. from NC Mts (DN 4), Ky (DN 4), Ill (DN 4), Kan (DN 4).

* **male, male hog** (see *boar hog*): Boar; used in the presence of women, not common. Reported from NC Mts (DN 4), Ky (DN 4), sInd (DN 3), seMo (DN 2), swMo (DN 5), nwArk (DN 3), Kan (DN 4), eNeb (AS 12.104, *male-pig*).

* **male horse** (see *stud, stud horse*): Stallion; used mostly in the presence of women, fairly common. Reported from wcWVa (AS 2.360), seMo (DN 2, *male brute*).

* **masons** (see *dirt-daubers, mud-daubers*): A kind of wasp; not common. VWB. NED (3.b) In the names of animals, esp. certain insects which build a nest of sand, mud, or the like; CD *mason bee.*

middlin, middlin meat (see *side meat*): Salt pork; common everywhere. VWB. Reported from eAla (DN 3), wcWVa (AS 2.360), seMo (DN 2), swMo (DN 5), Ozarks (AS 5.19, nwArk (DN 3). DAE (2) *American, S & SW*, 1777–1904; NED (4) *U.S.*, 1859 (Bartlett); CD (II.2) *West. and So. U.S.*

* **middling** (see *tolerable*): Fair, in answer to "how are you?"; common everywhere. VWB. NED (B.2) 1810–1894; CD (2) Not in good health, yet not very ill; also, in Scotland, in fairly good health, *Rural*; EDD (2) *Colloq.* in Sc, Irel, and Eng.

* **milk gap** (see *cow pen, cow pound, cuppen*): Pen for cows; in the southern part of the Blue Ridge.

(give someone) the mitten (see *kick, sack*): Jilt (someone); common. VWB *get the mitten*. Reported from wcWVa (AS 2.360) Ark (DN 5), nwArk (DN 3), Neb (DN 5), NY (DN 5), wNY (DN 3), Conn (DN 5), cConn (DN 3), Me (AS 5.124). DAE (2.a) To get the mitten, *colloq.*; (b) to give the mitten, *colloq.*, 1847–1902; T 1838–1855; NED (3) *Slang*, or *colloq.*, 1838–1884; CD *Colloq*; EDD Can.

* **moderate, moderate down** (see *abate, calm down, be laying, lower down*): Of the wind, subside; rare. Reported from wcWVa (AS 2.360), Western Reserve (DN 4), Cape Cod (DN 2), Me (AS 5.127). NED (1.b) 1678–1897; CD (II.1); EDD *moderate*, adj. (5) of the weather, calm, Sh.

mosquito hawk (see *snake doctor*): Dragon fly; on Chesapeake Bay. VWB. Reported from eAla (DN 3), seMo (DN 2), nwArk (DN 3). DAE *American, Southern*, 1737–1842; T; NED (2.b) *U.S.*; CD (1.A) *U.S.*

mud daubers (see *dirt daubers, masons*): Wasps; not common. VWB. Reported from nwArk (DN 3). DAE *American*, 1856–1899; T; NED (5.b) 1856–; CD A digger wasp.

* **new year's gift!**: Happy new year!; not common. Reported from eAla (DN 3), seMo (DN 2), nwArk (DN 3).

* **nicker** (see *whicker, whinny*): Noise made by a horse at feeding time; everywhere except south of the lower James. VWB. Reported from Va (DN 4), eAla (DN 3), Erie Canal (AS 6.99), sInd (DN 3), wInd (DN 3), sIll (DN 2), seMo (DN 2), swMo (DN 5), nwArk (DN 3). NED Chiefly *Sc.* and *north. dial.*, (1) 1774–1880; CD (1); EDD *Gen. dial.* use in Sc, Irel, and Eng.

oldfields colt (see *base-born, woods colt*): Illegitimate child; in the southern Piedmont. VWB *oldfield*, cleared land some distance from the house. DAE (2.a) *oldfield, American*.

* **ox** (see *gentleman cow, male, steer*): Bull; on the lower Rappahannock, in the presence of women.

paling fence (see *picket fence*): A fence made of pales, pointed slats; common everywhere. Reported from eAla (DN 3), seMo

(DN 2), nwArk (DN 2). DAE (1) 1806–1925; NED *paling* (4) 1805; EDD (1) Sc, Yks.

paper sack (see *poke*): A paper bag; not common. Reported from Va (DN 4), eAla (DN 3), sIll (DN 2), seMo (DN 2), nwArk (DN 2), Washington (DN 2), as "Westernism" (AS 1.152). DAE (II.8.b).

parlor (see *chamber, front room, living room, room, sitting room*): (a) A family living room, (b) a "best room"; common everywhere. DAE 1640–1923; NED (2) . . . Formerly often simply the "room" or "chamber," sometimes a bedchamber, 1374–1886; CD (3) . . . In Great Britain the common sitting-room or keeping-room of a family as distinguished from a drawing-room intended for the reception of company. In the U.S., where the term drawing-room is little used, parlor is the general term for the room used for the reception of guests; EDD (2) The inner room of a cottage or farmhouse of the ground floor, used either as a sitting or a bed-room: eYks, sYks, Lin.

patch (see *lot*): A field (of tobacco, etc.); common. VWB (2). Reported from sIll (DN 2), nwArk (DN 3). DAE *American* (1), 1653–1904; NED (2.b) 1577–1894; CD (6); EDD (4) Sc, Chs, nWil.

peckerwood: Woodpecker; in the Piedmont. Reported from Va (DN 4), Shenandoah Valley (AS 12.287), eAla (DN 3, *universal*), wTex (DN 4), South (DN 4), Ky (DN 5), So App Mts (AS 15.53), seMo (DN 2), Ozarks (DN 5, AS 15.53), nwArk (DN 3), central west (DN 5). DAE *American*, 1859 (Bartlett)—1909.

* **pert** (see *spry*): Lively; common everywhere. Reported from wcWVa (AS 2.361), SC (AS 18.67), Tenn (AS 18.67), sInd (DN 3, AS 16.24, AS 14.264), seMo (DN 1, DN 2), nwArk (DN 3), NY (AS 5.152). NED Since 17th cent. *dial.*, 1500–1889; CD (2); EDD Lakel, Lin, Hrf, Oxf, Bdf, Hmp.

picket fence (see *paling fence*): A fence made of pales, pointed slats; rare except among the cultured. Reported from App Mts (DN 5, *picketin fence*), Aroostook, Me (DN 3). DAE *American*, 1800–1917; NED (IV.7), 1857; CD.

* **piece, piece meal** (see *bite, snack*): A lunch eaten between meals; in the Blue Ridge south to the James. Reported from wInd (DN 3, *to piece*, eat between meals). NED (15.b) short for "piece of bread" (with or without butter, etc.), *spec.* such a bread eaten by itself, not with a regular meal, *Sc* and *Eng. dial,*

1787–1903; CD (4.f) *prov.* or *colloq.*; EDD (8) A slice of bread or bread and butter, etc., esp. that given to children and carried in the pocket, to be eaten as lunch; also *piece-time*, lunch-time, Sc.

pluck (see *hasslet*): The heart, liver, and lights of a sheep, ox, or other animal; east of the Blue Ridge, not common. VWB. Reported from Conn (DN 1). DAE (1) 1772–1873; NED (III.6) 1611–1904; CD (4) . . . also used figuratively or humorously for the like parts of a human being; EDD (11) *fig.*, of human heart and lungs.

plum (across) (see *clean across, clear across, jam across*): Entirely (across); in the southern part of the Blue Ridge. VWB. Reported from NC (DN 5), Barbourville, Ky (DN 3), Tenn Mts (DN 1), eAla (DN 3), sInd (DN 3), sIll (DN 2), Mo (DN 1, also familiar in Mich), nwArk (DN 3), eNeb (DN 3). DAE *Colloq.*, 1845–1925; T 1601–1893; NED (B.2.c) Chiefly *U.S. Slang*, 1587–1897; CD (3) *Colloq. U.S.*; EDD (8) *Obs.*

plunder: Household or personal effects, baggage; common everywhere except the Northern Neck and the Eastern Shore. VWB. Reported from Ohio River Valley (AS 9.320 household effects,—used figuratively sometimes for goods in general), eAla (DN 3), Tenn Mts (AS 14.91 *house plunder*), sIll (DN 2), seMo (DN 2), nwArk (DN 3), Wichita, Kan (DN 4), Me (DN 4), Sherwood's List of Provincialisms (DN 5). DAE *American* 1805–1856; T; NED (3) *U.S., Local,* 1817–1873; CD (1) *Local U.S.*

* **poke, paper poke** (see *paper sack*): A paper bag; west of the Blue Ridge. Reported from swPa (AS 7.20), wcWVa (AS 2.362), eKy (DN 3), Tenn Mts (DN 1), Tenn (AS 11.373), So App Mts (AS 15.45), seMo (DN 2), swMo (DN 5), nwArk (DN 3), Ozarks (AS 4.204, AS 5.427, AS 15.45), wTex (DN 4), Underworld Jargon (DN 5, pocketbook). NED Now chiefly *dial*, 1276–1902; CD (1) A pocket, pouch, bag, sack; EDD In gen. dial. use in Sc, Irel, and Eng, (1) a bag, sack; a wallet; a pocket.

pone (see *corn dodger, dodger*): A hard, hand-shaped cake of corn bread; common everywhere. VWB. Reported from Ga (DN 3), Fla (DN 3), wTex (DN 4), seMo (DN 2), swMo (DN 5), nwArk (DN 3), Neb pioneer English (AS 7.168, a thick pancake baked in a covered skillet). DAE *American, Southern,* (2) A patty or cake of corn or wheat bread, 1796–1903; NED Orig.

the bread of the North American Indians, made of maize flour in thin cakes, and cooked in hot ashes; now in southern U.S., any bread made of maize, esp. that of a coarse or poor kind; also very light bread, enriched with milk, eggs, and the like, and made in flat cakes, 1612–1861; (b) a cake or loaf of such bread, 1796–1887; CD *sw U.S.*

pone bread (see *corn bread, corn pone*): Corn bread; common everywhere. DAE *American*, cornbread in the form of pones, 1785–1833.

poor (see *puny, scrawny*): In poor health; common everywhere. VWB. Reported from wcWVa (AS 2.362, *porely*), Ind (AS 16.22), sInd (AS 14.264, *porely*), Martha's Vineyard (DN 5), Me (AS 2.80). DAE *American, Obs.*, 1758; T Nearly *obs.* in England, 1778–1878; NED *obs.*, 1758; CD (3.c); EDD gen. of live-stock: Sc, Cum, Yks, Chs, Der, War, Oxf, Sus, Som.

* **pretty day:** Pleasant day; common everywhere among all classes. Reported from Va (DN 1), Ill (DN 1, DN 4), New Orleans, La (DN 4), seArk (AS 13.6), nwArk (DN 2), Ia (DN 4), Kan (DN 4). EDD (4) Sus, Amer (DN 1).

primp up (see *dike up, fix up, prink*): Get dressed up; common everywhere. DAE *American*, 1881–1906; NED *dial.*, 1801–1880; CD (I); EDD Sc, nCy, Cum, Glo.

* **prink** (see *dike up, fix up, primp up*): Get dressed; not common. VWB Dress ostentatiously or fantastically. Reported from cConn (DN 3). NED (2.b) *colloq.*, 1709–1898; CD (I.1) To prank; dress for show; adorn one's self; II, *trans.*; EDD: Sc, nCy, Yks, Shr, Glo, eAn, Ken, Som Dev, Corn, Amer.

* **proud (to see someone):** Pleased (to see someone); common everywhere. Reported from eAla (DN 3), La (AS 11.368), wcWVa (AS 2.362), Ky (DN 4), NC Mts (DN 4), Tenn Mts (DN 1), Tenn (AS 11.373), seMo (DN 2), swMo (DN 5), nwArk (DN 2), cConn (DN 3), Sherwood's Provincialisms (DN 5). NED Early use (and still *dial.*), 1250–1593; EDD Clc, Cum, Chs, IW, Som, wCor; Amer.

pudding (see *hog's head cheese, souse*): A sausage of pig's entrails, cereal, etc.; fairly common. DAE 1859–; NED (I.1) Now chiefly *Sc.* and *dial.*, 1305–1819; CD (1); EDD (2) Sc, Sh I, Per, Fif, Dmf, Der, sDev.

* **pull flowers:** Pick flowers; common everywhere. Reported from eAla (DN 3, *universal*), sInd (DN 3), sIll (DN 2), Norse

dial. of Wisc (DN 2), nwArk (DN 3). NED (I.1.c) Now chiefly
Sc., 1340–1854; CD (2); EDD Sc, Ayr, Cum, Yks, nLin.

pull bone, pulling bone (see *lucky-bone, pully bone, wishbone*):
Wishbone; east of the Blue Ridge. DAE *American, local;* NEDS
(2) *U.S.*, 1906; EDD *pull bone,* wYks, *pulling bone* Shr.

*** pully bone** (see *lucky-bone, pull bone, wishbone*): Wishbone;
west of the Blue Ridge and in the southern Piedmont. Reported
from Va (DN 4), eAla (DN 3), wInd (DN 3), swMo (DN 5),
nwArk (DN 3), Ozarks (AS 8.51).

*** puny** (see *poor, scrawny*): In poor health; common everywhere. VWB. Reported from Va (DN 4), eAla (DN 3), Cumberlands (AS 7.191, AS 7.94 *puny-lookin'*), sInd (DN 3), seMo
(DN 2), swMo (DN 5), nwArk (DN 3), La (AS 11.368). T;
NED (4.c) 1866–1904; CD (2).

rail fence (see *log fence, worm fence*): Common everywhere except on the Eastern Shore. VWB *Rail.* Reported from nwArk
(DN 3, *railin fence*). DAE *American;* NEDS *U.S.*, 1649–1902.

reckon: Suppose; common everywhere among all classes.
VWB. Reported from eAla (DN 3), Miss (DN 4), Ky (DN 3),
wInd (DN 3), sIll (DN 2), seMo (DN 2), swMo (DN 5), nwArk
(DN 2, DN 3), Ozarks (AS 5.19, AS 5.428), cConn (DN 3). DAE
(1) To suppose, 1707–1917; (2) I reckon, used parenthetically
or as an affirmative reply, Eng. *dial.* and *southern U.S.*; T 1811–
1908; NED (6) 1513–1875; CD (6) ... Though regularly de-
veloped and used in good literature, has come to be regarded as
provincial or vulgar because of its frequency in colloq. speech in
some parts of the U.S., esp. the South; EDD: Sc, Eng, Amer.

*** red-worm** (see *angleworm, earthworm, fishing worm, ground
worm*): Earthworm; only west of the New River. Reported from
swMo (DN 5), nwArk (DN 3, *common*). NED 1450–1856.

*** rick.** A stack of hay, usually long and rectangular; common everywhere except the Tidewater south of the Rappahannock and the Eastern Shore. VWB. Reported from sIll (DN
2), seMo (DN 2, DN 5, also of wood), nwArk (DN 2, of wood;
DN 3, of hay, grain, or wood), eNeb (AS 12.106), nwLa (DN 4,
of wood). NED 900–1895; EDD sb. and vb., In Gen. dial. use
in Sc, Irel, and Eng for a stack of hay, Cum "a long pile."

*** rising:** A small boil; fairly common. VWB. Reported
from Va (DN 4), sIll (DN 2), seMo (DN 2), swMo (DN 5),
Ozarks (AS 5.20), nNH (DN 4), Me (DN 4). NED (11.b) Now
dial., 1563–1847; CD Now *colloq.*, or *dial.*; EDD wCy, Som.

(throw a) rock: (Throw a) stone; common everywhere. VWB A stone of any size larger than a pebble. Reported from Va (DN 4), eAla (DN 3), NC (DN 5, *to rock*), Barbourville, Ky (DN 3), Tenn Mts (DN 2), seMo (DN 1, *to rock*), swMo (DN 5, *to rock*), nwArk (DN 3, *to rock*), nwArk (DN 1), Ottawa, Kan (DN 2, *to rock*), cConn (DN 3), eMe (DN 3), Miss Intelligencer (DN 4), Sherwood's Provincialisms (DN 5), Dunglison's Glossary (DN 5). DAE (2) *local*, 1817–1882; NED (I.1.b) *U.S.* and *Austr.*, a stone of any size, 1700–1895.

rock fence (see *stone fence*): A fence of loose stone; everywhere, but not common north of the Rappahannock. Reported from eAla (DN 3), nwArk (DN 3), NY (DN 1). DAE (11) 1896 (DN 1).

(the) room (see *chamber, front room, living room, parlor, sitting room*): The living room; among older people, rare. NED See *parlor*; EDD (3) The best sitting-room: neCs, Cae, eSc, Slk, Dmf, sYks, eYks, sNot.

run (see *branch, creek*): A stream; in the Shenandoah Valley, the northern Piedmont, and the Tidewater north of the James. VWB. Reported from Va (AS 15.386–7: (1) a brook, (2) a creek or small river, (3) a bottom or meadow, (4) a canal, (5) a tributary of a stream, (6) the flow of a stream), Md (As 10.256–9, *most frequent in the mountains*), Ohio River Valley (AS 9.320), Cumberlands (AS 15.47), Great Smokies (AS 15.47), Ozarks (AS 8.51, AS 15.47), Dunglison's Glossary (DN 5). DAE (1) 1605–1908; NED (II.9) Chiefly *U.S.* and *north. dial.*, 1581–1877; CD (10); EDD (26) Lnk, nCy, nYks, nLin, Nrf.

* **sack (someone)** (see *kick, mitten*): Jilt (someone); fairly common. VWB. Reported from sIll (DN 2), seMo (DN 2), nwArk (DN 3), Ozarks (AS 5.20). NED (I.4) *Slang*, 1825–1902; CD (4) *Slang*.

sack (see *burlap bag, crocus bag, grass sack, guano sack, sack-bag, tow sack,*): A large bag made of coarse canvas; not common. Reported from Va (DN 4), swPa (AS 7.20), eAla (DN 3), sIll (DN 2), seMo (DN 2), nwArk (DN 2). DAE 1645–1912; NED (I.1) 1000–1864; CD (1); EDD Var. *dial.* uses in Sc, Irel, and Eng.

* **sack bag** (see *burlap bag, crocus bag, guano sack, sack, tow sack*): A large bag made of coarse canvas; rare. VWB A bag holding three bushels of grain.

sallet: Greens cooked for food; common everywhere except west of the Blue Ridge. VWB. Reported from Va (DN 4), wcWVa (AS 2.363), App Mts (DN 5, salad), So App Mts (AS 15.45, salad), seIll (DN 2), seMo (DN 2), Ozarks (AS 4.204, AS 15.45, salad), NY (DN 2), NE (DN 5, provincialism). DAE (1.b) *American, Southern*; NED *obs.* form of *salad*; CD *salad*, formerly also *sallet*, (2) herbs for use as salad: colloq. restricted in the United States to lettuce; EDD *sallet*: Edb, Yks, Lan, Chs, War, Wor, Shr, Hrf, Glo, Bch, Sus; *sallit*: Yks, eLan, seWor.

saw buck, wood buck, buck (see *saw horse*): A rack upon which wood is laid for sawing by hand; in the Shenandoah Valley, not common. DAE *American*, 1839–; NED (7) *U.S.*, 1860, Bartlett; CD (6.a), also called *sawhorse, U.S.*

saw horse, wood horse, horse (see *saw buck*): A rack upon which wood is laid for sawing by hand; common everywhere. VWB. Reported from Canada (DN 1). DAE 1848–1920; NED *saw horse* (d) 1778–1883, *horse* (L.7.b) 1718–1769; CD; EDD *saw horse* wYks, Wil, Amer, *horse* wSom.

scrawny (see *poor, puny*): In poor health; fairly common. VWB. DAE *American*, mean, meager, thin, 1833–1897; NED *U.S.*, variant of *scranny*, 1833–1883; CD A *dial.* form of *scranny* now prevalent.

* scrooch down, scrutch down: Crouch down; common everywhere. VWB. Reported from Va (DN 4), eAla (DN 3), NC (DN 1), wInd (DN 3), swMo (DN 5), Kan (DN 4), Neb (DN 3), West Brattleboro, Vt (DN 3), Me (DN 4). NED *dial.* and *U.S.*, 1882–1911; EDD: Yks, Not, Amer.

scuttle, coal scuttle (see *coal hod*): Coal hod; common everywhere. Reported from wNY (DN 3), cNY (DN 1, *coalscuttle*). DAE 1833–1889; NED (2.b) 1849–1909; CD *coalscuttle*; EDD (2) A shallow wooden or wicker basket for produce or corn, occasionally coal: Cum, Yks, Lan, Der, Not, Lin, Lei, War, Oxf, Bdf, eCy, Suf, sCy.

shades (see *blinds, curtains*): Roller shades for windows; regularly in the Piedmont, less commonly elsewhere. DAE *American*, 1645–1889; NED (III.11.a) *U.S.*; CD (10); EDD (6) eDur, nYks, wYks, Amer.

* sheaf (see *bundle*): Fairly common west of the Blue Ridge and on the Middle Neck. NED (1) 725–1862; CD; EDD.

shindig (see *breakdown, frolic, hoedown*): A party; common everywhere. VWB A ball or dance; especially with much uproar and rowdyism. Reported from eAla (DN 3, an entertainment),

wTex, (DN 4, an entertainment), wcWVa (AS 2.364), Ky (DN
1), swMo (DN 5, *shinadig*), nwArk (DN 3, an entertainment),
Neb (DN 3, a dance or party; a row), Neb pioneer English (AS
8.48), Mich (DN 1), wNY (DN 3, an entertainment) cConn
(DN 3, any public or social entertainment). DAE *American*,
Slang, (2) 1873–1911; NED *U.S.* 1859 (Bartlett)—1899; CD
Western U.S., *shindy*, a row or rumpus, *Slang*.

shock (see *hay cock, hay doodle*): A pile of hay in the field
at haying time; common everywhere. VWB. Reported from
Western Reserve (DN 4), sInd (DN 3), sIll (DN 2), nwArk
(DN 3). DAE shock of corn, *American*, 1863–1920; NED; CD;
EDD gen. *dial.* and *colloq.* use in Sc and Eng.

(get) shut of (someone): (Get) rid of (someone); common
everywhere. Reported from Shenandoah Valley (AS 12.287),
wcWVA (AS 2.355), NC (DN 4), Tenn (DN 4, also from Tenn
Mts), seO (DN 4), wInd (DN 3), sIll (DN 2), Ill (DN 4), seMo
(DN 2), swMo (DN 5), Kan (DN 4), Neb (DN 4), Sherwood's
Provincialisms (DN 5).—T; NED *dial.* and *colloq.*, 1500–1892;
CD *prov.* Eng. and U.S.; EDD gen. *colloq.* use.

side meat (see *middlin*): Salt pork: in the Blue Ridge and south
of the lower James. Reported from eAla (DN 3), seMo (DN 2),
nwArk (DN 3). DAE *American* 1873–1912; NEDS *U.S.;*
CD (1.12.b) *Colloq., western U.S.*

simlin: A kind of squash having a scalloped edge; common everywhere. VWB *cymblin*, a small eatable gourd. Reported from
seMo (DN 2, a small kind of squash), nwArk (DN 3, a bitter
gourd, mock melon . . . sometimes mistaken for a melon). DAE
cymbling, *American*, 1804–1911; NED *U.S.*, 1794–1896; CD (2)
A kind of small squash *S. and W. U.S.;* also *simnel* (1) a rich
sweet cake offered as a gift at Christmas and Easter and Mothering
(Simnel) Sunday; (2) a variety of squash . . . resembling the cake:
now called *simlin, So. U.S.;* EDD A rich cake.

sitting room, setting room (see *chamber, front room, living room,
parlor, room*): A living room; common everywhere among all
classes. Reported from Hampstead, NH (DN 3). DAE 1771–
1925; NED 1806–1894; CD.

skillet (see *spider*): Now a cast iron frying pan, formerly a three
legged, long handled pan for use in the fireplace; common in the
western Piedmont and westward, scattered elsewhere. VWB Of
brass, cast not beaten, a semi-globe in form, having three short,

straight legs of about three inches in length cast on its bottom. The handle is tapering but flat and quite straight . . . only suitable to be used with a wood fire on the hearth. Reported from Tenn Mts (DN 1, a fry-pan with legs), eAla (DN 3, with three legs, and a cover, for baking), sIll (DN 2, *skillit*, any kitchen utensil), seMo (DN 2, a shallow iron vessel with a cover, used for baking). DAE (1) A cooking utensil having a long handle: (a) a small saucepan having three or four legs, *Obs.;* (b) a frying pan, 1630–1917; NED (1) A cooking utensil of brass, copper, or other metal, usually having three or four feet and a long handle, used for boiling liquids, stewing meat, etc.; 1403–1866; CD (1); EDD gen. *dial.* use in Sc, Irel, Eng, and Amer.

slop bucket: Garbage pail; common everywhere. Reported from Va (DN 4, *slop*), eAla (DN 3). DAE *slop-basin, slop-bowl;* NED (6) 1856; CD A pail or bucket for receiving slops or soiled water.

smear case (see *clabber cheese, cottage cheese, curd, home-made cheese*): Cheese made of the drained curd of sour milk; west of the Blue Ridge. Reported from the English of the Pa Germans (AS 10.169), Ohio River valley (AS 9.319), nwArk (DN 3). DAE *American*, 1829 (Royall, *Pennsylvania:* "A dish, common amongst the Germans . . . is curds and cream. It is very palatable, and called by the Germans smearcase")—1894; NED *U.S.* 1848 (Bartlett)—1893; CD See *cottage cheese.*

smouch (see *buss*): Kiss; fairly common everywhere. VWB. Reported from Tenn Mts (DN 1). NED 1575–1825; CD *Obs.* or *prov.* Eng.; EDD: nCy, Yks, Lan, Chs, Der, Lin, Lei, Nhp, War, Wor, Hrf, eAn, Sur, Dor, Amer.

snack (see *bite, piece*): A lunch eaten between meals; common everywhere. VWB. Reported from eAla (DN 2), wcWVa (AS 2.364), Ky (DN 5, a light, cold repast, originally a Gypsy cant term, meaning a share or division of plunder), eKy (DN 3), Tenn Mts (DN 1, also *snack-houses*), wInd (DN 3), nwArk (DN 3). NED (4.b) 1757–1874, also *snack-houses;* CD (3); EDD Sc, Irel, Eng, and Amer.

snake doctor (see *mosquito hawk*): A dragon-fly; common everywhere except on Chesapeake Bay and west of the New River. VWB. Reported from eAla (DN 3). DAE *American* (1) 1862–1899; NED (11.b); CD *Local, U.S.*

snaps, snapbeans (see *green-beans, string beans*): String beans;

common everywhere. VWB. Reported from Va (DN 5), eAla (DN 3), wcWVa (AS 2.364), nwArk (DN 3). DAE *snap bean, American*, 1775–1910.

snits: Apples cut in quarters and dried; in the northern part of the Blue Ridge, rare. Reported from the Shenandoah Valley (AS 12.287, slices, of oranges, etc.), wcWVa (AS 2.364, apples quartered for drying or for apple butter), Kan (DN 4, pieces of fruit quartered and dried). DAE *American, Local,* from Pa German *schnitz,* sections of apple, slices of dried fruit, 1848–1903.

*somerset: A somersault; common everywhere. Reported from eAla (DN 3), wNY (DN 3), Hampstead, NH (DN 3). NED 1596–1874; CD.

*song ballad, song ballet: Used with various meanings: a folksong or ballad, or the actual manuscript copy of it; not common. Reported from Va (DN 4, a song or ballad), Miss (AS 4.87, a manuscript copy of a song; in the So Appal meant a written copy made by children), wcWVa (AS 2.348: (1) the words of a song (2) a ballad or old song), swNC (DN 1, *song-valet,* the words of a song), Cumberlands (AS 7.94, the long-hand copy of the words of a ballad), So App Mts (AS 15.50, ballad), Ozarks (AS 15.50, ballad), southern negroes (AS 3.213, an elaboration of an older folk song . . . mostly written by negroes), NJ (AS 12.231, by negroes). NED *ballad* 1492–1855; EDD (1) A song, a ballad; sometimes applied to the sheet upon which several songs are printed: Cum, Yks, Lan, Chs, Der, Nhp, War, Shr, Hrf, Brks, Ess, Ken, Sus, Wil, Som, Dev.

souse (see *hog's head cheese, pudding*): Pig's feet, ears, etc., either pickled or jellied. VWB (pickled). Reported from nwArk (DN 3, a jellied compound, a great delicacy). DAE 1805–1895; T; NED Now *dial.* and *U.S.*, the various parts of a pig, prepared for food by means of pickling, 1391–1872; CD (2) The head, ears, and feet of swine pickled; EDD (6) The ears, feet, tail, etc., of a pig pickled: nCy, Nhb, Cum, Yks, Chs, Der, Not, Lin, War, Glo, Brk, Suf, Hmp, IW; also *souse-cheese.*

spicket: Faucet; in general use everywhere. VWB The inner plug of a wooden tap. NED *Obs.,* 1530–1725; CD . . . any plug fitting into a faucet used by drawing off liquor; EDD in *comb.,* Sc, Nhb, Dur, Lan, Chs, Shr.

spider (see *skillet*): Now a cast iron frying pan, formerly a three legged, long handled pan for use in the fireplace; in the Tidewater area and on the Eastern Shore. VWB. Reported from Miss (DN 3), nwLa (DN 4), Ill (DN 3), Mo (DN 3), Neb pioneer English (AS 7.169), NY (DN 3), cConn (DN 3), Cape Cod (DN 2, a frying pan with high sides), Vt (DN 3), Me (DN 5), Aroostook, Me (DN 3). DAE (2) *American*, An iron frying pan or skillet, sometimes provided with long legs, 1790–1905; NED A kind of frying pan having legs and a long handle; also loosely, a frying-pan, *Orig. U.S.*, 1830–1869; CD (4) A cooking utensil having legs or feet to keep it from contact with the coals: named from a fancied resemblance to the insect . . . the ordinary frying-pan is, however, sometimes erroneously termed a *spider*.

*spry (see *pert*): Lively; common everywhere. VWB. Reported from nwArk (DN 3), cConn (DN 3), Miss Intelligencer (DN 4, as a Yankeeism), Humphrey's Glossary (DN 5). T 1815–1846; NED Current in English dialects, but more familiar as an Americanism, 1746–1892; CD *Prov. Eng.* and *U.S.;* EDD In gen. *dial.* and *colloq.* use in Sc, Eng, and Amer.

*squall (see *gully-washer*): A hard storm, mostly wind; not common. VWB A sudden shower of rain or snow, not necessarily accompanied by wind. NED (1) A sudden and violent gust, a blast or short sharp storm, of wind (Orig. *Naut.*), 1719–1886; CD A sudden and violent gust of wind . . . usually accompanied by rain, snow, or sleet.

*stairsteps: Stairway; common everywhere among all classes. Reported from eAla (DN 3, *universal*), NY (DN 1), Chicago people of NE antecedents (DN 3).

*steer (see *gentleman cow, male, ox*): A bull; on the Eastern Shore, on the lower Rappahannock, and in the southern Piedmont, in the presence of women.

stone fence (see *rock fence*): A fence of loose stone; on the Middle Neck, in the Piedmont north of the Rappahannock, and the lower Shenandoah Valley. DAE (1) 1682–1905.

*stout: Strong; common everywhere. VWB Broad and strong. Reported from scPa (DN 4), sIll (DN 2), Ozarks (DN 5), nwArk (DN 3), cNY (DN 3), wConn (DN 1), seNH (DN 4). NED (A. II.6) Strong in body, of powerful build, *?Obs.*, 1386–1842; (b) in robust health, strong . . . *Obs. exc. Sc.*, 1697–1884; CD (4) Hardy, vigorous, lusty; (5) Firm, sound . . . strong; EDD Var. *dial.* uses in Sc, Irel, Eng, and Amer; (1) strong; healthy; well-grown; convalescent.

string beans (see *green-beans, snaps*): North of the Rappahannock, not common. DAE *American,* 1759–1891; NED (32) *U.S.,* 1842; CD.

stud (see *male horse, stud horse*): Stallion; common everywhere. VWB. Reported from eAla (DN 3), nwArk (DN 3), New Brunswick (DN 1), Dunglison's Glossary (DN 4). DAE *American* (1) 1803–1891; NED (4.b) *U.S.* 1803–1891; CD (3) *Colloq.*

*****stud horse** (see *male horse, stud*): Stallion; fairly common everywhere, a breeders' term. VWB. Reported from eAla (DN 3), Aroostook, Me (DN 3). NED 1000–1891; CD.

sundown: Sunset; common everywhere. VWB. Reported from eAla (DN 3), sInd (DN 3), sIll (DN 2), seMo (DN 2), nwArk (DN 3), NJ (DN 1), wNY (DN 2), Me coast (AS 3.139), early New England words (AS 15.230). DAE (1) 1712–1906; T 1796–1878; NED (1) Chiefly *U.S.* and Eng. and Colonial *dial.,* 1620–1896; CD (1); EDD: Abd, Rxb, Gall, Ir, Yks, nLin, War, Wor, Glo, Nrf, Som, Dev; Amer, Austr.

sunup: Sunrise; common everywhere, mostly among older people. VWB. Reported from Cumberlands (AS 7.94), eAla (DN 3), sInd (DN 3), sIll (DN 2), seMo (DN 2), nwArk (DN 3), NJ (DN 1), Me coast (AS 3.139). DAE 1712–1901; T; NED *Local,* chiefly *U.S.,* 1847–1899; CD *local, U.S.;* EDD also *sunbreak.*

take up: *Of school,* begin; not common. Reported from Va (DN 4), wcWVa (AS 2.365), Western Reserve (DN 4), nwArk (DN 3). DAE (10.e) 1876–1903; NED (90.s) *trans.,* to begin afresh, 1604–1902; CD.

*****toad frog** (see *dry-land frog, hop toad*): Toad; not common. Reported from Va (DN 4), eAla (DN 3, *universal*), La (DN 4), NC (DN 4), Cumberlands (AS 7.94, a tailless, jumping amphibian, resembling the frog and often mistaken for a toad), sIll (DN 2), seMo (DN 2), Ozarks (DN 5, either a toad or a frog), nwArk (DN 3), Kan (DN 4).

*****tolerable** (see *middling*): Fair, in answer to "how are you?"; common everywhere. VWB. Reported from eAla (DN 3), Ky (DN 1), sInd (AS 14.264), seMo (DN 2, *universal*), swMo (DN 5). NED (5.b) 1847; CD (4) *colloq.;* EDD; wCy, Dev, and Amer.

tote: Carry (a load) in one's arms or on one's back or shoulders; common everywhere. VWB. Reported from the South (AS 8.23, not from WVa), eAla (DN 3), Miss (DN 4), La (DN 5), w-Tex (DN 4), eKy (DN 3), NC (DN 5), seMo (DN 2), swMo

(DN 5), Ozarks (AS 5.429), eMe (DN 3). DAE *American*, chiefly *southern*, 1677–1920; T 1676–1892; NED *U.S. colloq.*, 1676–1892; CD *So. U.S., colloq.* or *prov.*, also humorous use in the North and West.

*touchous (see *ashy, wrathy*): Easily angered; common everywhere. VWB. Reported from eAla (DN 3), Ky (DN 1), seMo (DN 2), swMo (DN 5), Ozarks (AS 4.204). EDD: Irel, Nhb, Lakel, Cum, Yks, Lan, Chs, Der, Amer.

tow sack (see *burlap bag, crocus bag, grass sack, guano sack, sack, sack bag*): A large bag made of coarse canvas; in the Norfolk area. DAE *tow* 1646–1842; NED *tow* 1530–1896, *tow cloth* 1822; CD *tow;* EDD *tow:* Sc, Irel, Nhb, Wm, Yks, eAn.

*trumpery (see *lumber*): Junk; on the Middle Neck, rare. Reported from West Brattleboro, Vt (DN 3). NED (2) 1531–1807; CD (3); EDD (2) Sc, Irel, Yks, Hrt, Wil, Dor, Som, Cor.

turn (see *armful, load*): The amount (of wood, etc.) that can be carried by a person at one time; everywhere, but not common in the southern part of the Blue Ridge. VWB. Reported from NC (DN 5), SC (DN 6), eAla (DN 3), La (DN 1), wcWVa. (AS 2.366), nNH (DN 4, of water), Me (DN 4, of water), Aroostook, Me (DN 3, two pailfuls, of water). DAE (2) 1800–, *dial.;* NED (VII.37) A measure of various commodities, the quantity dealt with at one "turn" or stroke of work, 1805–1905; CD (19); EDD (7) As much as is done or fetched with one return—two ridges in plowing, two pitchers of water: Sus, Hmp, IW, Cor, Amer.

turn of corn (see *grist*): The amount of corn taken to (or from) the mill at one time; common everywhere except in the Shenandoah Valley and the Tidewater area. VWB. Reported from eKy (DN 3, about two bushels), Ky (DN 4), Tenn Mts (AS 14.92), NC Mts (DN 4), seMo (DN 2), swMo (DN 5). DAE 1800–1896.

*turn out (see *let out, break up*): Of school, be over; everywhere, but not common north of the James. Reported from Ga (DN 3), Fla (DN 3), Ind (AS 17.130, *turn over*), nwArk (DN 3, *universal*). NED (75.g) *trans.*

*(to have) weather: (To have) bad weather; not common. VWB. Reported from Va (DN 1), sIll (DN 2), seMo (DN 2), nwArk (DN 3), Tex (DN 1), wTex (DN 4), Sarah Orne Jewett (DN 2). CD.

*(to) weather: To storm; not common. Reported from swMo (DN 5), Tex (DN 1). EDD: nYks.

weskit (see *jacket*): A vest; common among older people. Reported from Va (AS 6.100). DAE *waistcoat* (2) 1640–1912; NED *Colloq.* or *vulgar*, 1519–1869; EDD An undercoat worn by either sex: Kent, Yks, Dev.

*****whetrock** (see *whetstone*): Whetstone; mostly in the southern part of the Blue Ridge, and the southern Piedmont. Reported from Va (DN 4), eAla (DN 3), Ky (DN 4), NC Mts (DN 4), Ill (DN 4), nwArk (DN 3).

whetstone (see *whetrock*): In the northern Piedmont and in the Tidewater. DAE 1643–1923; NED (1) 725–1896; CD (1); EDD: Nhb, Cum, Yks, Chs, Lei, Som, Dev.

*****whicker** (see *nicker, whinny*): Noise made by a horse at feeding time; on the Tidewater and Eastern Shore. VWB. Reported from NC (DN 5), eAla (DN 3), sInd (DN 3), sIll (DN 2), swMo (DN 5), nwArk (DN 3). NED (2) 1808–1912; EDD: Sc, Wm, Yks, Glo, Brks, Hmp, IW, nCy, Wil, Dur, Som, Amer.

*****whinny** (see *nicker, whicker*): Noise made by a horse at feeding time; scattered on the Eastern Shore and in the Shenandoah Valley. NED (1) 1530–1894; CD; EDD To cry, as a child.

wishbone (see *lucky-bone, pull bone, pully bone*): Fairly common among younger people. VWB. Reported from eNeb (AS 12. 104). DAE *American*, 1853–1905; CD.

*****woods colt** (see *base-born, oldfields colt*): An illegitimate child; west of the Blue Ridge. Reported from wcWVa (AS 2.366), Winchester, Ky (DN 1), Tenn Mts (AS 14.92), Nc (AS 18.68), NC Mts (DN 4), SC (AS 18.58), Ind (AS 16.25), seMo (DN 2, a horse or person of unknown paternity), swMo (DN 5), nwArk (DN 3), Me (AS 5.124).

worm fence (see *log fence, rail fence*): A zigzag rail fence; fairly common in the northern Piedmont and on the Eastern Shore. VWB. Reported from Va (DN 4), swMo (DN 5), Aroostook, Me (DN 3). DAE *American*, 1652–1913; T 1817–1867; NED (IV.f) *U.S.*, 1796–1842; CD.

wrathy (see *ashy, touchous*): Angry; common everywhere. VWB. Reported from eAla (DN 3), nwArk (DN 3), cConn (DN 2). DAE *American, Low colloq.*, 1828–1900; T 1834–1888; NED *Orig.* (and chiefly) *U.S.*, 1828–1887; CD *colloq.*; EDD: Sc, Irel, Brks, IW, Amer.

THE SECRETARY'S REPORT

A. THE CHICAGO MEETING

The annual meeting was held in Chicago at the Stevens Hotel, December 27, 1945, 2:00–3:30 P. M. The meeting was well attended, more persons being present than could be seated. Although there was discussion of each paper, a number of persons told the Secretary or later wrote him that they felt that the meeting had not had enough time allotted to it to allow for unhurried presentation of papers and full discussion of them.

The following papers were read:

"Some Observations on Eastern Canadian Dialect," Henry Alexander, Queen's University, Ontario.

"Some Questions and Opinions on Place-Name Study," Frederic G. Cassidy, University of Wisconsin.

"In the Wake of the *DAE*," M. M. Mathews, University of Chicago.

Reports were given by the Secretary and the President. The Auditing Committee sent in its report, which stated that the Secretary's bookkeeping was correct.

The officers recommended for 1946 by the Nominating Committee were elected. The principal officers are: President, Kemp Malone, Johns Hopkins University; Vice-President, Atcheson L. Hench, University of Virginia; Secretary-Treasurer, George P. Wilson, Woman's College of the University of North Carolina. Members of the Executive Council are: Kemp Malone, Johns Hopkins University; Atcheson L. Hench, University of Virginia; George P. Wilson, Woman's College of the University of North Carolina; Harry Morgan Ayres, Columbia University; Hans Kurath, Brown University; Stith Thompson, Indiana University; Albert C. Baugh, University of Pennsylvania.

The next meeting will be held in Washington, D. C., in conjunction with the Modern Language Association.

B. SOME MATTERS REPORTED ON AT THE MEETING

1. *Deceased members.* The President of the Society asked that the group rise and remain silent a few moments in memory of four

members who had died during the year: Professor B. J. Vos, Dr. Thomas A. Knott, Dr. John L. Lowes, and Dr. C. C. Rice.

2. *Work of committees.* The Secretary commended the marked industry and achievements of two chairmen and the members of their committees: Dr. Margaret M. Bryant, chairman of the Committee on Proverbial Sayings; and Dr. I. Willis Russell, chairman of the Committee on New Words. He expressed the hope that other committees would show similar results now that the war is over.

3. *Activities of individual members.* The following is a paragraph from the Secretary's report as read: "During the year I learned that so many members had written articles and books and had engaged in other valuable activities that I thought it would be of interest to all members if I made a report on these doings. Accordingly, in October I sent a form letter to each member requesting that if he had 'committed' any good acts, he cognize me of them. I stand before you a poor psychologist and a frustrated man: only three persons responded to my request. In his *Supplement I to the American Language* Mr. Mencken concludes a discussion on our Society and its members in these judgmatical words: 'Thus the society stands in the first years of its second half-century, rejuvenated and indeed reincarnated. It is still small, but its members include all American philologians who are really interested in American English, and it has more ambitious plans than ever before.' I hope that in *Supplement II* Mr. Mencken will add that our members are too modest to testify to their good deeds."

4. *"Indecent" material.* The Secretary raised the question as to whether so-called "indecent" dialect and proverbs should be collected and published by the Society. All who voiced their opinions thought that such material should be collected and published.

5. *Membership.* During the year several members were good enough to send in the names of persons who later joined the Society. Those who have been most helpful in this respect are: Dr. James F. Bender, Dr. Margaret M. Bryant, Dr. Josiah Combs, Dr. Thomas A. Kirby, Miss Mamie J. Meredith, Dr. Robert Price, and Dr. Francis Utley.

Here are some figures on our membership for 1945:

Life	18
Members paid through or beyond 1945	156
Members paid through 1944	25
Unpaid but probably good	58
Libraries	122
Exchange and complimentary	8
Total	387

6. *Financial report.* This report is as of December 15, 1945.

Receipts

Money brought over from last year	$746.33
Dues from persons	411.00
Dues from libraries	304.00
Gifts: A. W. Read and C. L. Barnhart	5.00
Sale of *Needed Research in American English*	.25
Sale of *PADS* No. 1	2.75
Sale of *PADS* No. 2	21.62
From Ency. Brit. Co. for new words	100.00
Interest on money in bank, June 30	4.44
Total	$1595.39

Disbursements

For 1000 envelopes (6½ x 9½)	$3.83
" express	1.18
" miscellaneous	8.20
" paper	4.44
" postals and stamps	57.09
" *PADS* No. 2	325.35
" *PADS* No. 3	169.45
" secretarial work	4.50
" stencils	1.19
Total	$575.23
Balance on hand	$1020.16

7. *Change of address.* The Secretary would be most grateful to all members who change their address if they would notify him immediately of their full new address. Such an act of charity would save time, energy, postage, and copies of *PADS*.

THE AMERICAN DIALECT SOCIETY

Membership in the Society is conferred upon any person interested in the activities of the Society. Dues are $2.00 a year for persons or institutions. Members receive free all publications. The price of any issue when purchased separately will depend upon the production cost of the issue.

The *Publication of the American Dialect Society* is issued at intervals during the year.